Biblical Worship

Text Book Series

Biblical Worship

*God has always had a way
He wants to be worshiped*

Shamblin Stone

WestBow
PRESS
A DIVISION OF THOMAS NELSON

WestBow Press books may be ordered through booksellers or by contacting:

WestBow Press
A Division of Thomas Nelson
1663 Liberty Drive
Bloomington, IN 47403
www.westbowpress.com
1-(866) 928-1240

Scripture taken from the New King James Version. Copyright © 1982 by Thomas Nelson, Inc. Used by permission. All rights reserved.

Cover artwork by Larry DeTienne ©2011 The Worship College All Rights Reserved

ISBN: 978-1-4497-3713-9 (sc)
ISBN: 978-1-4497-3714-6 (hbk)
ISBN: 978-1-4497-3712-2 (e)
Library of Congress Control Number: 2012900664

Printed in the United States of America

WestBow Press rev. date: 03/08/2012

"It is only when men begin to worship that they begin to grow."

Calvin Coolidge,
thirtieth president of the United States

Table of Contents

List of Illustrations..xi
List of Tables xiii

Preface: *My Call to Teach Worship* 1

Chapter One: *What Is God Doing in the Earth Today?*................. 7
Jesus Christ Is the Central Figure of History................................7
Jesus Christ Is the Creator of All that Exists 8
History Is "His-Story".. 10
Arise, Shine.. 11
To Whom Is Isaiah Writing These Five Chapters?.......................14
Righteousness and Praise..17
Why Both Righteousness and Praise?... 20
The End-Time Contrast... 21
How Will God Establish Righteousness and Praise? 23
A Crown of Glory.. 27

Chapter Two: *God's Response to Non-Biblical Worship* 29
Christian/Biblical Worship Is 29
God Has Always Had a Way He Wants to Be Worshiped 29
Worship Is the Expression of Our Hearts................................... 30
Christian Worship Is Based on Love..31
Worship and Blood Sacrifices... 32
The Story of Cain 34
Self-Willed Worship vs. Biblical Worship................................... 36
The "Way" of Cain... 36
The Three Deadly Sins of the Last Days According to Jude 37
These Sins in the Church Today 39

Chapter Three: *Biblical Synonyms for Worship* 41
Worship Is a General Term with Many Synonyms.......................41
The Difference between Synonyms and Expressions 42
Some Biblical Synonyms for Worship...................................... 43

Chapter Four: *Defining Biblical Worship* 45
Why Learn Definitions?... 45
Important Information for This Chapter 46
Greek Words
Proskuneo 46
Other Greek Words 49
Hebrew Words
Halal 51
Other Hebrew Words 60

Chapter Five: *Intimate, Passionate Worship*............................. 65
God Desires an Intimate Relationship with Mankind 65
Biblical Relationships between God and Man 67
Jesus Creates Every Person Out of Love.................................... 68
The Father/Child Relationship 69
Relationships Are to Progress and Develop 69
Progression into a Marriage Relationship with God................... 70
The Marriage Act and the Worship Act 71
Passionate Worshipers Are Passionately Obedient...................... 73
The Results of Non-Passionate Obedience.................................74
A Word of Balance 77

Chapter Six: *The Presence of God* 79
Psalm 100—An Exposé of Biblical Worship 79
Worship Springs from a Thankful Attitude 80
God's Goal for Us Is that We Would Know Him........................ 83
How to Know God.. 84
Practicing the Presence of God 85
The Desire for God.. 88
Isaiah's Revelation of God... 90
The Worship Cycle 93
Let's Review—Worship Is ….. 93
Two Philosophies of Worship.. 94

Chapter Seven: *Rejoice Always—A Study of When to Worship*.. 99
Rejoice Is a Synonym for *Worship* 99
Worship Is Easy When Life Is Good.. 99

Why Do We Suffer? 100
Job's Struggles 101
Habakkuk's Struggles 103
Habakkuk's Resolve 106
What Does it Truly Mean to Rejoice? 106
Why Dancing? 107
God Dances 108
Jesus Danced 109
A Result of Exuberant, Extreme Rejoicing 110
Other Results of Biblical Rejoicing 113

Chapter Eight: *Perfected Praise* 116
Make His Praise Glorious 116
Man's Natural Definition of Perfected Praise 117
God's Definition of Perfected Praise 118
The Setting of Perfected Praise 119
The Children Who Offered Perfected Praise 121
Perfected Praise Summarized 122
Comfortable Life Philosophies 123
God's Greatest Commandment 123
The Religious Response to Perfected Praise 125
Perfected Praise Is Ordained Strength 126
The Reason God Ordained Strength through Extreme Worship 127
Lucifer, God's Enemy 127
Lucifer's Punishment 128
Mankind Is Part of Satan's Punishment 128
High Praises 129
Hebrew Parallelism 131
Parallelism in Psalm 149 132
The Kingdom of Satan 133
To Execute Punishments 135
The Written Judgment 137
This Honor Have All His Saints 139
Concluding Thoughts 140

About the Author, *Pastor R. Shamblin Stone* 141
About the Worship College 143
Bibliography 145

List of Illustrations

Preface

Shamblin Stone in 1973 1

Shamblin Stone in 2006 4

Shamblin Stone in 2007 5

Chapter 6

Romans 1 and Psalm 100 Staircase 81

The Rain Cycle 93

The Worship Cycle 93

Chapter 8

Eastern House 132

About the Author

Pastor Shamblin and Chris Stone in 2011 141

About the Worship College

The Worship College logo 143

List of Tables

Chapter 1

Table 1: The Two Realms of Creation 9

Table 2: Comparing Two Scriptures 15

Table 3: Exegesis of Isaiah 64:5 by Phrases................................... 19

Chapter 2

Table 4: World Religions/Christianity Comparison 32

Table 5: The Prominent Sins of the Last-Days Church............... 38

Table 6: The Outcome or Consequences of These Sins............... 39

Chapter 3

Table 7: Biblical Synonyms for Worship.. 43

Chapter 5

Table 8: Biblical Relationships with God 67

Chapter 6

Table 9: Come Before His Presence 80

Table 10: Backsliding will Touch Every Part of our Beings!...... 82

Table 11: John's Outline of Christian Growth............................. 84

Table 12: Two Philosophies of Worship—Table A...................... 95

Table 13: Two Philosophies of Worship—Table B 95

Table 14: Two Philosophies of Worship—Table C...................... 96

Chapter 7

Table 15: Habakkuk's Condition.. 105

Chapter 8

Table 16: Two Perspectives on Life.. 123

Table 17: The Three Levels of Satan's Punishment 133

Table 18: Demonic Chain of Command...................................... 137

Preface

My Call to Teach Worship

After receiving a church music and vocal music degree in 1977, I traveled full-time as a singer/songwriter, waiting on my first big record deal. Performance was all I knew back then, and I was good enough at it to have shared concert stages with most of the then-known Christian artists. I was also known by most of the Christian record labels at that time and was actively courting two or three of them. I was confident that it was just a matter of time before the world would become familiar with the music of Shamblin

Shamblin Stone in 1973

Stone. However, God intervened in my life to make sure that did not happen.

I still remember the very first time God confronted me with His call for my life. It was at a Wednesday night concert at the Church of God in Fairbury, Nebraska in the sweltering month of July 1979. The intense, three-hour routine I followed to set up my sound system was only about half complete. The church's air conditioner had gone out that day—too late for them to get a repairman—and there was no fan to be found.

Into this volatile setting walked the innocent pastor's wife, excited that I had brought my road show back to their town. "Hi, Shamblin Stone," she called out as she approached with her hand extended as a welcoming gesture. On my knees, hard at work, I quickly raised my head to see who was there. At that moment, the perspiration from my forehead gushed into both of my eyes, causing them to sting. Blinded, I reached for my handkerchief to wipe my eyes, leaving the pastor's wife with her hand extended. I regained my sight in time to see her withdraw her hand awkwardly after several minutes of waiting.

We engaged in a few minutes of small talk; then she asked me a very important series of questions. "Do you remember when you were here last year," she asked with a serious tone in her voice, "how you led us all into worship in the middle of your concert?"

I had to think about it for a moment. In those days, I never planned a concert. I always depended on God to tell me, while I was singing one song, what song He wanted me to do next from my repertoire. As I recalled my past concerts, I realized that, in every concert, God had led me to lead the audiences into singing songs of praise and worship they were familiar with. "Yes, I guess I do," I responded.

"Are you going to lead us into worship again tonight?" she continued.

Unsure how to respond to her—but based on the recent review of my memories of concerts—I answered, "I suppose I will."

"That will be great." She smiled. "I will look forward to that!"

It was a blow to an up-and-coming songwriter's ego to find out that the most memorable part of a past concert was the time of worship I led. "What about all of those wonderfully crafted songs I performed?" I thought to myself.

After the concert that night, the pastor's wife continued our conversation. "Since my husband is the pastor here, he has asked me to lead the worship."

"That's great," I said.

"No, it's not," she quickly responded. "I don't know anything about worship! I know music, but I've come to realize that knowing music is not the same thing as knowing worship."

I had never heard that concept before, and I was really not that interested in it, since my career was aimed at performance. But then came the question which would be the call of God to me for the rest of my life.

"Could you teach me how to lead worship the way you do?" she asked, blotting a tear from the corner of her eye.

How could I teach her anything? I knew nothing about worship. All I did was sing the songs God directed me to sing. That's all I knew to do.

I looked at her and said, "All I do is follow the leading of the Holy Spirit. Surely you can do that."

I don't remember when I finally realized how rude that comment was to her, but I know now that I have never apologized to her, nor have I thanked her for speaking as the oracle of God to me that night.

In those days, I was doing an average of seventeen to twenty concerts a month. For the rest of that July, all of August and September, and most of October, I had the exact same questions asked of me everywhere I went to sing. People asked whether I remembered leading worship the last time I performed for them, if I was going to lead worship, and if I could teach them about worship.

After a month or so of this happening, I became prideful and smug about my emerging sense of worship leading. Yet, I still had no intentions of figuring out how to help these untrained worship leaders. I saw them as only distractions to me in my pursuit of a performance career.

About the third week of October, I showed up at an independent church in Salina, Kansas. This time, it was the pastor of the church who came in as I was setting up my PA. "Do you remember," he began, "when you were with us about a year ago?"

"Yes, I do," I answered confidently, already expecting his questions.

"Well," he proceeded, "do you remember leading us into worship in the middle of your concert?"

"I sure do," I smugly answered, feeling superior from the dozens of times I had experienced this same conversation in churches all across North America in the last few months.

"Well," he continued somewhat tentatively, "were you planning to lead us in worship in your concert tonight?"

"I imagine so," I boasted from my false sense of confidence.

"I'd rather you wouldn't!" the pastor requested.

I paused what I was doing, feeling like I had been struck in the stomach by a professional fighter. "Why? I don't understand," I responded through my shattered ego. "Did I do something to offend you or your church?"

"No. You don't understand," the pastor responded. "Last year, you led us into a depth of worship we had never experienced before."

"Well, praise God!" I cut in.

"But you don't understand," he continued. "You packed up your PA and left town!" The pastor's voice was showing signs of frustration and borderline anger. "We have been trying for the entire past year to obtain that level of worship which you led us into and have not been able to reach it. So, if you are planning on leading us in worship again and not teaching us how we can obtain that level of worship ourselves when you leave, then thanks, but no thanks!"

For the first time in my life, as I stood before that congregation to sing, I felt empty. I realized I had been trying to give my audiences what I wanted them to have—my "great" songs—instead of what God wanted them to have—His presence, which comes when He inhabits our praise.

The entire following week, I lay across my bed, weeping from this revelation and the emptiness I felt because I was unable to help these churches with their worship. After several days of desperately crying out to God, repenting for my arrogance and pride, and telling God I was sorry for asking Him to bless my ideas rather than asking Him for His ideas for my life, God spoke to me. "God," I wept, "I know nothing about worship, so how can I help these churches with their worship?"

"I know about worship," God quietly assured me, "and if you let me, I'll teach you."

"I wouldn't know where to begin to read in the Bible to have you teach me," I argued.

"But I know," said the Lord. "Are you ready to let me teach you? Are you ready to give up your ideas for mine? Are you ready to lay down your will for mine?"

"Yes, Lord. I surrender … all!"

Thus began the daily revelations from God's Spirit and the Bible about worship. My career became a lifetime of helping churches and individuals to understand worship as God intended, thereby making it possible for them to obtain a greater depth of worship and God's presence. I changed from seeking recognition as a Christian star

Shamblin Stone in 2006

to desiring with all my heart to serve others by helping them worship their God the way He wants to be worshiped.

In 1979, the Lord told me that He was about to raise up men and women all over the world with revelations on worship and that He had chosen me to be one of them. He told me He would only give me 10 percent (at the most) of His revelation on worship. Therefore, if I wanted a more complete understanding of worship, I would have to share what God gave to me with others, and they would have to share their revelations on worship with me. At no time, He assured me, would He ever give any one person a complete revelation of worship, meaning we would have to share what He had given us with each other for any of us to have a more complete picture of what He said concerning worship at this time in church history.

The book *Biblical Worship* is the first installment of the knowledge about worship which God has given to me in a revelation. As I have taught this material in class settings all over North America, I have noticed that God uses it to open up each student to his or her own revelation from God about worship. You should expect this as you go through this book. When you receive revelation from God about worship, share it with me, please! I want the most complete picture of biblical worship I can have here on earth, and I will need the revelations God gives you about worship in order for my picture of worship to be complete.

Shamblin Stone in 2007

Chapter One

What Is God Doing in the Earth Today?

Jesus Christ Is the Central Figure of History

According to the calendar that you and I use, all of world history is referenced around Jesus Christ. We reference the years before Christ came to earth by counting backward. We indicate these dates with a *BC* after them, which stands for "before Christ." An alternative acronym which is being used by secular society in the recent years is BCE. This is thought to indicate the phrase "Before the Common Era," therefore taking the reference to Christ out of our current dating system.

The years after Christ came to earth are counted forward, and are preceded by the initials *AD*. This represents the Latin phrase *anno domini*, which means "in the year of our Lord." Those wishing to exclude Christ from our day to day lives have adopted the use of CE instead of the AD. This is believed to represent the words "Common Era."

However, according to the internet based encyclopedia Wikipedia at http://en.wikipedia.org/wiki/Common_Era, these abbreviations "BCE" and "CE" have been used throughout history since the 1600's to mean "Before the Christian Era," and "Christian Era."

Every time we write a date on anything, we are acknowledging that "Jesus the Christ is Lord" over that year. When this happens, Jesus is praised, even if we don't want Him to be praised. Atheists and agnostics in the world still give praise to Jesus every time they open their calendars to check their schedules for the day. There is no way of getting past the fact that all of history revolves around our Lord Jesus Christ.

Jesus Christ Is the Creator of All that Exists

Jesus is the creator and designer of the universe and the world we live in. This includes both the physical and spiritual realms.

> "For by Him were all things created, that are in heaven, and that are in earth, visible and invisible, whether they be thrones, or dominions, or principalities, or powers: all things were created by Him, and for Him." (Colossians 1:16 KJV)

The spiritual realm is represented in this Scripture in Colossians in the words *heaven* and *invisible*. The physical realm, which we can see, touch, and experience, is represented by the words *earth* and *visible*.

There are also four more things listed here that are divided into these two categories of God's creation: *thrones, dominions, principalities,* and *powers*.

Let's look at the first two of this list, *thrones* and *dominions*. In the earth, we have thrones, which represent the rulers of various countries or kingdoms. We also have the kingdoms that these rulers rule over. These are called dominions. North of the border of the United States is a country which we refer to as the Dominion of Canada. In most cases, these kingdoms of the world are divided into nations of people who reside in a particular land space.

Now let us consider the last two items listed: *principalities* and *powers*. These are identified for us in Ephesians 6 as part of the hierarchy found in the demonic spiritual realm.

> "For we wrestle not against flesh and blood, but against principalities, against powers, against the rulers of the darkness of this world, against spiritual wickedness in high places." Ephesians 6:12 KJV

For visual learners (of which I am one), let me summarize Colossians 1:16 with this chart.

The Two Realms of Creation
according to Colossians 1:16

Spiritual Realm	Physical Realm
1. heaven	1. earth
2. invisible	3. visible
4. principalities	5. thrones
6. powers	7. dominions

Table 1

The first realm, represented in the first column, is the Spiritual Realm. It includes both the godly part of this spiritual realm, as well as the demonic aspects of it. God created all of these spiritual beings. It was their choice to become evil, not God's. The second column of our chart deals with what we can see with our natural eyes here on earth.

God created both of these realms. You and I exist (live) in both of these realms simultaneously. This is evidenced by the fact that God made mankind to have both a spirit and flesh. This allows us to experience both of these realms at the same time. As Christians, the only way we should seek to know and experience the spiritual realm around us is through our Creator, Jesus Christ. Any other avenue into the spiritual realm is strictly forbidden, according to the Word of God.

> *"There shall not be found among you any one that makes his son or his daughter to pass through the fire, or that uses divination, or an observer of times, or an enchanter, or a witch, or a charmer, or a consulter with familiar spirits, or a wizard, or a necromancer. For all that do these things are an abomination unto the LORD: and because of these abominations the LORD your God does drive them out from before you." (Deuteronomy 18:10–12, KJV).*

History Is "His-Story"

Down through the ages, God has been at work in the lives of mankind. His primary purpose has always been to redeem us back into a loving relationship with Himself and to restore lost truths to His people.

Over the course of my life, I have been privileged to travel extensively in ministry to all types of churches across almost all denominational lines. I have also been exposed to many different missionaries who have traveled to the four corners of the globe. I have always made a point of asking every Christian leader I've met in my travels and everyone returning from their mission field this question: "What is God doing *with* you, or saying *to* you, at this particular time?"

I have been amazed to learn that, invariably, God seems to deal with His church around the world about the same things at the same time. This has been verified over and over in my experiences. I would leave a Baptist church in one city and drive two hundred miles to minister in a Pentecostal church in another city. Neither of these churches knew the other. Over supper that night, I would hear the Pentecostal pastor tell me that God was doing the exact same things in their church that the Baptist pastor had told me about over breakfast. This would be exactly what a Methodist pastor and a Nazarene pastor had told me the week before. Over and over, I have verified this phenomenon throughout my ministry.

God seems to move around the world in seasons. Over my lifetime, I can remember several distinct seasons the Lord has taken the church through. Although I was not born until the late 1940s, I still remember the season of "hope in heaven" born out of the despair of the Great Depression. The catch phrase of that season was "by and by," which showed up in many of the songs of that era. Here are lyrics from just a few of those songs:

> ➢ "By and by, when the morning comes …"
> ➢ "We'll understand it better by and by."
> ➢ "By and by, we're going to see the King."
> ➢ "In the sweet by and by, we shall meet on that beautiful shore."
> ➢ "When I die, hallelujah, by and by, I'll fly away."

Please understand that I am in no way trying to create an exhaustive list of seasons which God has taken the church through since the 1930s. It is only my intention to mention a few of these seasons in order to make my point.

One of the most recognized seasons which God brought His church through in this past century happened in the 1970s. The charismatic movement circled the globe, touching every known Christian denomination. Does that mean that every Christian in every church embraced this? Of course it doesn't. However, because of that season, there has developed a world-wide tolerance and acceptance of the New Testament gifts of the Holy Spirit, including speaking in tongues. Before that season, there was great hostility toward these gifts.

Another season we passed through in the 1990s was a season of spiritual manifestations, including laughter. Some of the names you may remember from that season include Rodney Howard Brown, the Toronto Blessing, Brownsville, Smithson, etc. This season did not last much past the end of the '90s; nevertheless, it circled the globe as something God was teaching His people for that time.

I realize there have been abuses of all of God's seasons, but that does not negate the fact that God moves upon the worldwide church simultaneously to restore us back to His truths.

Toward the very beginning of the 1980s, God began giving people around the world fresh biblical revelation regarding worship. This season seems to be continuing and gaining momentum, even to this present day. I personally feel that this season of the restoration of biblical worship will continue to crescendo until the day Jesus returns to earth. Here's why I believe that.

Arise, Shine

This is what I consider to be one of the most important Scriptures in the entire Bible about worship. It is also one of the Scriptures God has used to verify His call on my life.

> *"For as the earth brings forth its bud, as the garden causes the things that are sown in it to spring forth, so the Lord GOD*

will cause righteousness and praise to spring forth before all the nations." (Isaiah 61:11, NKJV).

Before we examine the message of this Scripture, I would like to look at its context.

Isaiah wrote a fairly long book over the course of his lifetime. Anyone who has read the book of Isaiah can almost always pick out the places in it where he lunges into a new thought or topic. It is obvious that a span of time has passed since he has written anything, but he took up the pen again with a fresh revelation from God.

One such break occurs between Isaiah 59 and 60. The first verse of Isaiah 60 reveals to us an explosive new topic on Isaiah's heart—worship and letting God's glory be revealed through His people:

"Arise, shine; for your light has come! And the glory of the Lord is risen upon you" (Isaiah 60:1, NKJV).

To *shine* is to reflect God's glory in much the same way the moon reflects the glory of the sun. In this analogy, we are the moon, and God is the sun. Just as the moon has no light of its own, neither do we contain our own light. Just as the moon must be in the right position to reflect the light of the sun, so do we need to get into position, or proper relationship, to reflect God's glory. We are commanded to "arise," to get into position, to get into relationship with the source of our light—Jesus Christ.

There is also a sense of urgency in this command for us to arise and shine, revealing that timing is very crucial. As I read this Scripture, it feels like God is saying, "I am doing something in the earth right now that I haven't done before, so I need you to get in position for it, or else you may miss what I'm doing." History is full of the reports of people who missed what God was doing at a particular time. One of these reports would certainly be when God came to earth in the form of a man—Jesus Christ.

"He came to His own, and His own did not receive Him" (John 1:11, NKJV).

Throughout history, it seems that, many times, the people who experienced the prior season of God and received the previous revelation from God have become the biggest opponents of the present season of God.

This theme of praise and glory continues for several chapters in Isaiah until chapter 64. Here are some of the references to this subject which I extracted from these five chapters.

> "But the Lord will arise over you, and His **glory** will be seen upon you ... and they shall proclaim the **praises** of the Lord ... but you shall call your walls Salvation, and your gates **Praise** ... that I may be **glorified**". (Isaiah 60:2b, 6b, 18b, 21b, NKJV).

> "To give them beauty for ashes, the oil of joy for mourning, the garment of **praise** for the spirit of heaviness; that they may be called trees of righteousness, the planting of the Lord, that He may be **glorified** ... I will greatly rejoice in the Lord, my soul shall be joyful in my God ... so the Lord GOD will cause righteousness and **praise** to spring forth before all the nations." (Isaiah 61:3b, 10a, 11b, NKJV).

> "You shall also be a crown of **glory** in the hand of the Lord, and a royal diadem in the hand of your God ... You who make mention of the Lord, do not keep silent, and give Him no rest till He establishes and till He makes Jerusalem a **praise** in the earth." (Isaiah 62:3, 6b, 7, NKJV).

> "I will mention the lovingkindnesses of the Lord and the **praises** of the Lord ... You, O Lord, are our Father; Our Redeemer from Everlasting is Your name." (Isaiah 63:7, 16b, NKJV).

> "For since the beginning of the world men have not heard nor perceived by the ear, nor has the eye seen any God besides You, Who acts for the one who waits for Him. You meet him who **rejoices** and does righteousness, Who remembers You in Your ways." (Isaiah 64:4–5 NKJV).

I would love to take the time to exegete all these Scriptures; alas, we must reserve that for another day and stay focused on our task. My purpose for including these Scriptures here was simply to give you a quick glimpse at the context of the Scripture we do need to exegete.

However, there is still one more question we need answered before we can turn our attention to Isaiah 61:11.

To Whom Is Isaiah Writing These Five Chapters?

This can appear as an oversimplified question. We all know the Bible is written to "whosoever will" read it and believe it. Perhaps the better question to ask would be, "To what time period is Isaiah writing?" The answer to this question is found within the chapters themselves. Here is the first of two "bookend" Scripture clues surrounding Isaiah 61:11:

> "The sun shall no longer be your light by day, nor for brightness shall the moon give light to you; but the Lord will be to you an everlasting light, and your God your glory. Your sun shall no longer go down, nor shall your moon withdraw itself; for the Lord will be your everlasting light, and the days of your mourning shall be ended." (Isaiah 60:19–20, NKJV).

I am very sure these events have not yet taken place on the earth, or else we would have read about them in our history books; better yet, we would still be experiencing them today. When are these events scheduled to take place in human history? If we find the answer to this question, we will find out to whom Isaiah has written these five chapters.

The book of Revelation at the end of our Bible is clearly identified as being written to the end of time for this world. John was taken up into heaven and shown what will take place when our world as we know it is coming to an end. Here is how God called John up to heaven and the reason he was granted that visit:

> "After these things I looked, and behold, a door standing open in heaven. And the first voice which I heard was like a trumpet speaking with me, saying, 'Come up here, and I will show you things which must take place **after** this'" (Revelation 4:1, NKJV).

The entire book of Revelation after chapter 4 is devoted to what takes place "after this"—at the end of the age. Toward the end of this book of Revelation, we have a very interesting Scripture passage:

"The city had no need of the sun or of the moon to shine in it, for the glory of God illuminated it. The Lamb is its light. And the nations of those who are saved shall walk in its light, and the kings of the earth bring their glory and honor into it. Its gates shall not be shut at all by day (there shall be no night there). And they shall bring the glory and the honor of the nations into it." (Rev. 21:23–26, NKJV).

When we hold this Scripture in Revelation up next to the last Scripture we read from Isaiah, it becomes very apparent that both Scriptures are talking about the same things, which are to take place at the end of the age.

Comparing Two Scriptures

Isaiah 60	Revelation 21
The sun shall no longer be your light by day	*The city had no need of the sun or of the moon to shine in it*
Nor for brightness shall the moon give light to you	*... or of the moon ...*
But the Lord will be to you an everlasting light	*for the glory of God illuminated it. The Lamb is its light*
[11] Therefore your gates shall be open continually; They shall not be shut day or night	*Its gates shall not be shut at all by day (there shall be no night there).*
[11] That men may bring to you the wealth of the Gentiles, And their kings in procession.	*the kings of the earth bring their glory and honor into it*
And the days of your mourning shall be ended.	*[4] And God will wipe away every tear from their eyes; there shall be no more death, nor sorrow, nor crying. There shall be no more pain*

Table 2

What are the odds that two men writing about 750 years apart from each other could describe this exact same scene, pointing out six of the same unexpected events? Both of them had to have received glimpses into the future of the same timeframe and scene. Since we know that John is describing an end time event, we must conclude that Isaiah was also writing to the people living in the end times of man's history.

In case you are not totally convinced of who Isaiah is writing to in these five chapters, let's look at the other "bookend" Scripture I mentioned earlier:

> "Behold, the LORD hath proclaimed unto the end of the world, Say ye to the daughter of Zion, Behold, thy salvation cometh; behold, His reward is with Him, and His work before Him" (Isaiah 62:11, KJV).

The phrase "proclaimed unto the end of the world" is extremely important to the understanding of the people to whom the Lord is proclaiming His message. My first thoughts, after reading this, assigned the word "end" a geographical meaning. After all, it makes sense that the Lord wants to proclaim His message to every part of the world—the "ends" of the earth.

After a long time of interpreting this Scripture this way, I finally decided to look the word up to verify what I was thinking. I was shocked to find out the end in this Scripture did not reflect geography at all, but rather, chronology. Here is the definition:

> **Strong's Hebrew Number 7097, Hebrew word: qatseh kaw-tseh', 1d** at the end of (a certain time)

By putting this Scripture together with the one we examined and compared to Revelation, it becomes crystal clear that Isaiah is writing these five chapters to the end time people of God.

My purpose here is not to define eschatology for us, and I am very aware of the varying views on this subject within the body of Christ. However, if we choose to avoid all discussion of the end times, we will miss out on what God is trying to say to us here in Isaiah. Is it too much to ask us all to consider that we who are alive now are at least living closer to the end times than any other generation in history? Therefore, these five chapters in Isaiah apply to us more than any previous generation.

I personally believe that we are living in the final days of man's history. Furthermore, I believe that, in these last days, the season God has chosen for us is the establishing of righteousness and praise over all the earth.

> "For as the earth brings forth its bud, as the garden causes the things that are sown in it to spring forth, so the Lord GOD will cause **righteousness** and **praise** to spring forth before all the nations." (Isaiah 61:11, NKJV).

Righteousness and Praise

I said earlier that these five chapters in Isaiah deal mainly with the establishing of praise over the earth in the last days. God has sensitized me to the subject of praise and worship by making it my life's message. However, I must be fair to the Scriptures here and report to you that, in this last season of history, God will also establish righteousness at the same time He establishes praise.

In 1979, God started talking to me about the subject of establishing praise and worship throughout the whole earth. Since that time, God has implemented a revival of righteousness among His people. We have seen the secret sins of many Christian leaders exposed to the whole world. Things which used to be kept secret have come out, causing a renewed reverence to rise within the entire body of Christ.

Let me share with you the Scriptures from these same five chapters in Isaiah that deal with righteousness.

> "I will also make your officers peace, and your magistrates righteousness. Violence shall no longer be heard in your land, also your people shall all be righteous." (Isaiah 60:17–18, 21, NKJV).

> "That they may be called trees of righteousness, the planting of the Lord, that He may be glorified. For I, the Lord, love justice; I hate robbery for burnt offering; I will direct their work in truth. For He has clothed me with the garments of salvation, He has covered me with the robe of righteousness ...

*For as the earth brings forth its bud, as the garden causes the things that are sown in it to spring forth, so the Lord GOD will cause **righteousness** and praise to spring forth before all the nations." (Isaiah 61:3b, 8, 10–11, NKJV).*

*"For Zion's sake I will not hold My peace, and for Jerusalem's sake I will not rest, until her **righteousness** goes forth as brightness, and her salvation as a lamp that burns. The Gentiles shall see your **righteousness**, and all kings your glory. And they shall call them the Holy People, the Redeemed of the Lord." (Isaiah 62:1–2, 12, NKJV).*

*"Who is this who comes from Edom, with dyed garments from Bozrah, this One who is glorious in His apparel, traveling in the greatness of His strength?–I who speak in **righteousness**, mighty to save.' For He said, 'Surely they are My people, children who will not lie.' Your holy people have possessed it but a little while." (Isaiah 63:1, 8, 18, NKJV).*

*"You meet him who rejoices and does **righteousness**, Who remembers You in Your ways. You are indeed angry, for we have sinned–In these ways we continue; and we need to be saved. But we are all like an unclean thing and all our **righteousnesses** are like filthy rags; we all fade as a leaf, and our iniquities, like the wind, have taken us away." (Isaiah 64:5–6, NKJV).*

I have come to believe that there can be no true biblical worship in our lives until there is true pursuit of righteousness and holiness. Worship ceases to be biblical when there is no righteousness accompanying it. Holiness is beautiful when joined to worship.

"O worship the LORD in the beauty of holiness: fear before Him, all the earth" (Psalm 96:9, KJV).

In fact, our shining, referred to in Isaiah 60:1, seems to be the result of both our worship and righteousness. Read Isaiah 62:1 again to verify this:

"For Zion's sake I will not hold My peace, and for Jerusalem's sake I will not rest, until her righteousness goes forth as brightness, and her salvation as a lamp that burns."

We do well to remember one thing at this point. Any brightness that comes from us does not originate with us. We simply reflect the glory of God. It is He who puts righteousness on us as a garment.

"For He has clothed me with the garments of salvation, He has covered me with the robe of righteousness," (Isaiah 61:10, NKJV)

Here is a promise we should memorize from our text chapters in Isaiah. Summarized, this promise simply states that God will reveal His presence to those who worship Him in the context of righteousness.

"You meet him who rejoices and does righteousness, who remembers You in Your ways." (Isaiah 64:5, KJV)

Exegesis of Isaiah 64:5 by Phrases

You meet him	To meet with God is to enjoy His presence
who rejoices	To rejoice in God is to praise Him
and does righteousness	We are incapable of doing righteous things by ourselves, just as the moon is incapable of shining without the sun. "Christ in us" is the only hope we have of showing His glory. (Colossians 1:27).
Who remembers You in Your ways	Once we have experienced God's presence, we will never forget it. We will crave it. We will desire it as an addict desires drugs.

Table 3

Why Both Righteousness and Praise?

Why are these two items incomplete without the other? The answer can be given in one word—balance. Much of what God has created functions best in balance with something else: ebb and flow, night and day, male and female, beginning and end, tension and release, hot and cold, sound and silence, life and death, light and dark, etc. Righteousness and praise are simply another duality added to this incredibly long list of life balances.

For some of these balances, we can state the absolute co-existent position of balance—there cannot be one without the other. Others we define using an understanding definition of duality—we would not know one as well without the other. For instance, we would not know and appreciate heat as well without cold. We would not know and appreciate light and all it does to enhance our lives without darkness. Likewise, we would not understand and appreciate salvation as much if there was no such thing as sin.

Righteousness and praise can actually be defined using both descriptions of duality. There can be worship without righteousness, and there can be holiness without praise; but there is no biblical balance. In other words, we cannot know true biblical worship without also knowing and experiencing godly holiness. We can't truly know one without the other. If we try to do this, we develop a distorted sense of both righteousness and praise.

Holiness without the relationship and intimacy of worship is quickly reduced to rules and regulations—dos and don'ts. This type of righteousness can become more external than internal. Before we know it, holiness becomes more about the way we look than the state of our hearts. It becomes more of an act of our willpower and less of a byproduct of our loving relationship with Jesus. It becomes the way we have to be to deserve the title of Christian, rather than the way we are becoming by spending time with Jesus. Righteousness without praise is dry, and it is a lot of hard work.

Worship without holiness becomes sloppy and self-centered, rather than Jesus-centered. Praise for the sake of praise is not focused on the object of our praise—Jesus—but deteriorates into self-gratification. We must have holiness as part of the motivation for our worship; otherwise, we lose sight of the fact that worship and praise are for God, not us. Of course, we experience many benefits when we worship God, not the least of which would be the presence of God; but what we receive when we worship is of only a distant secondary consequence. The real reason we worship God is because He deserves our praise.

Throughout church history, the body of Christ has developed a skewed understanding of righteousness and praise. However, we have now approached the time in history when God will restore proper balance to our understanding and practice of both righteousness and praise. I hope you are as excited about that as I am.

The End-Time Contrast

We have seen that the Lord will establish righteousness and praise "before all the nations" in the earth's final days. Does that mean this will happen to both the non-Christians and Christians alike? The answer to that is, not at the same time. What God is doing in His church is not necessarily what will happen in the rest of the world. Remember, we began by talking about different seasons God takes His *church* through. What Isaiah 61:11 tells us is that this season of righteousness and praise will be evident to all the nations. However, that doesn't mean the world will understand what is going on.

> "For the time has come for judgment to begin at the house of God; and if it begins with us first, what will be the end of those who do not obey the gospel of God? (1 Peter 4:17, NKJV).

In the last days, we will come into a time when the true, worshiping church will be in stark contrast to what the world looks like. This is explained for us in Isaiah 60:2:

> "For behold, the darkness shall cover the earth, and deep darkness the people; but the Lord will arise over you, and His glory will be seen upon you." (Isaiah 60:2, NKJV)

When I was ready to give my wife her engagement ring back in 1972, I went to a local jeweler in Wichita, Kansas who custom-made all his jewelry. He explained that there were two steps to designing an engagement ring. First, I would pick out the diamond; secondly, I would decide on a design for the gold ring itself. He asked me how much money I had to spend on the ring, then selected a very small envelope from his safe containing eight to ten unset diamonds.

Reaching under the counter, he brought out a thick, black velvet cloth cut into a square. He placed this cloth on the glass countertop about two feet away from me and proceeded to place a couple of the diamonds on the black cloth. Next to the rich black velvet, the stones sparkled like they were on fire.

"Which one of these do you like?" he asked me.

After a few minutes of looking at each of the stones through a jewelry magnifier, I finally made my decision. He picked up the one I had rejected with his tweezers and placed it on the glass counter next to the black pad. Then he put a third diamond on the black cloth and asked me the same question again. I couldn't believe it. The beautiful stone I had just been gazing at on the black cloth all but disappeared on the glass. What was the problem? There was no contrasting background for the diamond on the glass. However, the rich black velvet provided the optimum contrast, which made the diamonds seem to sparkle even more than ever.

By the way, the reason the jeweler put the black pad two feet away from me was so he could place the cloth directly under a bright spotlight shinning down on the counter from the ceiling. Those diamonds did not have any light of their own to shine with. It was only when they got into the perfect position—or relationship with the light—and they were displayed against a total contrasting substance that they sparkled so brightly.

So it will be with us in the last days. The contrast God places us up against is the world and the people of the world.

> "For behold, the darkness shall cover the earth, and deep darkness the people" (Isaiah 60:2 NKJV).

The original King James Version of the Bible uses a measurement adjective to describe the type of darkness that will settle on the people of the earth in the last days. Instead of "deep" darkness, it tells us that "gross" darkness will cover the people of the earth. It is important that we do not interpret this word as slang, as we would today. "Gross" is a unit of weight. When the Bible tells us that this type of darkness will cover the people of the earth in the last days, it is referring to a heaviness or oppression of darkness in the earth. What do you think? Does that describe the condition of our time, and its people? I believe it does.

How Will God Establish Righteousness and Praise?

"For as the earth brings forth its bud, as the garden causes the things that are sown in it to spring forth, so the Lord GOD will cause righteousness and praise to spring forth before all the nations" (Isaiah 61:11, NKJV).

There are two similar ways listed here which tell us how God will bring about the establishment of righteousness and praise in His church in the last days: *"as the earth brings forth its bud and as the garden causes the things that are sown in it to spring forth."*

The buds of the earth come forth every spring. Spring follows winter—the bleakest, coldest, most desolate of the four seasons. During winter, there is no sign of vegetative life. The trees are only forms which once supported life. When we look at a tree in winter, we see no promise that life will return to beautify the earth. There are only memories of when life ruled that tree. What makes winter easier to endure is the memory of past springs, when life has been evidenced all around us.

While waiting for the Lord to establish worship and holiness in your home church, remember any times in the past when He has revealed Himself to you. Maybe you weren't around during the times the older people talk about when God moved so mightily, but base your hope for His glory to be revealed in your life and in your church on the previous seasons of God's visitation. If you have to read books about the way God has moved in the past to stir up this hope in you for the glory of God, then do it. Ask the older folks to tell you stories about when God moved in the past. Don't be fooled by the bleakness and dryness of the current state of worship within your church. Hope in God, and ask Him to hasten this season in which His glory will be revealed in all the earth.

"I have set watchmen on your walls, O Jerusalem; they shall never hold their peace day or night. You who make mention

of the Lord, do not keep silent, and give Him no rest till He establishes and till He makes Jerusalem a praise in the earth." (Isaiah 62:6, NKJV).

It is all right to be dissatisfied with the state of worship in your local church, but don't "bail out" on your church until you have taken up the responsibility God has called you to—to be a watchman on the wall of your church. What are the watchmen to do?

1. Never hold their peace, day or night
2. Not keep silent
3. Give the Lord no rest

How long are you to function as a watchman in your church? *Till He establishes and till He makes Jerusalem a praise.* You do not have the right to abandon your church until you have spent time asking God to establish it in "Biblical Worship." In other words, don't complain about the worship of your church, pray about it! Keep praying until you see God establish your church as a "praise" to Him in your city! Keep praying until God establishes your church in "Biblical Worship."

Righteousness must be established within the hearts and lives of people. It is not something that happens automatically. Biblical worship is formed from obedience to the Lord's command to "Arise, shine." The people of God are made a praise in the earth when they obey God's command to praise Him.

Never complain to other people in your church about the state of the worship there! Function as the watchman you were placed there to be!

The second way God will establish righteousness and praise is found here.

"As the garden causes the things that are sown in it to spring forth..." (Isaiah 61:11, NKJV)

The onomatopoeia of the word *spring* in the phrase "spring forth" produces an exciting mental image of a flower opening using time-lapse photography. It denotes rapidness in its development. It conjures up the mental image of Jack's (from *Jack and the Beanstalk*) massively developed stalk which reaches high into the heavens after growing overnight. Most of us would be very happy if the worship in our churches developed like that. However, if we have that mental image, we will be greatly disappointed.

I'm not a very good gardener. I don't think I have much patience for it, but I have always admired those who have successful gardens of any type. I have observed several steps in the development of a good garden:

1. Prepare the ground
2. Plant the seed
3. Fertilize the seed/plant
4. Water the seed/plant
5. Clear the weeds
6. Protect the plant as it develops
7. Harvest the new seeds for next season's planting
8. Plant the best seed next season

Let me discuss these steps one at a time.

1. Prepare the ground

If you want your church to be open to improving its worship, you have to help its people realize there is a need for this before you introduce a change to them. They have to see the need before they will be open to having the need met.

2. Plant the seed

Jesus has made it clear to us in the Bible that the seed being sown is the Word of God.

> "Now the parable is this: the seed is the word of God" (Luke 8:11, KJV).

Plant the seed of worship in your church by sharing with fellow church members what the Bible says about it. If you only share your disgruntled attitude about worship, you will not be planting the right seeds. I guarantee you will not like that crop when it comes up.

3. Fertilize the seed/plant

This is encouragement. Always express appreciation for the state your worship is in. Always show appreciation for those involved in your worship, no matter where they are in their development process.

4. Water the seed/plant

Fund your worship development. Do not be stingy with your resources. A plant can have the best seed, but if you don't water that seed, it will not grow.

5. Clear the weeds

The cares of this world will grow up quickly and try to choke out your worship. You must not let that happen. Make worship of Jesus the priority of your life.

6. Protect the plant as it develops

Put a fence around your worship, with a big sign that says, "Keep off!" Your worship of Jesus is directed to Jesus, not other people. No one has the right to judge your worship, especially while it is vulnerable and in the developmental stage.

7. Harvest the new seeds

As you begin to understand God's heart regarding worship, He will give you further revelation about worship, which you need to share with others.

8. Plant the best seed next season

Instill into the next generations God's truths about worship.

The way God will establish righteousness and praise before all the nations in these last days will be through a process which will last all season long. Do not be discouraged if your church is not yet where God wants you to be. If we are faithful and obedient to "arise and shine," the day will come when God will have established His church as a praise and a tree of righteousness.

A Crown of Glory

> *"You shall also be a crown of glory in the hand of the Lord, and a royal diadem in the hand of your God." (Isaiah 62:3, NKJV).*

The ultimate result of God establishing righteousness and praise is for us to become a crown of glory in God's hand. We become this as we obey the command to arise and shine.

You may ask, "Aren't crowns and diadems made to be worn on the head as a symbol of position and authority? Why, then, are we said to be in His hand?" It is because God will have made His worshipers His crown of His glory. He will use His hand to bring His glory and authority to the whole earth. Let us give Him no rest until He does this in you and me and in our churches.

Chapter Two

God's Response to Non-Biblical Worship

Christian/Biblical Worship Is ...

Christian/biblical worship is the expression of mankind's love to our creator, God, in the ways He wants to be worshiped.

God Has Always Had a Way He Wants to Be Worshiped

It is presumptuous for mankind to think we can determine the best way to express our worship to God. It is, therefore, necessary for us to find out how God wants to be worshiped in order for our worship to be accepted by Him. To learn how God wants to be worshiped, we must turn to His Word, the Bible.

Why do we not look in the Koran to find how God wants to be worshiped, or in Buddha's writings, or the book of Mormon? The answer to this question is simple. The only way God wants to be reached by mankind is through Jesus. He Himself told us this with His very words, as recorded by John the apostle.

> "Jesus said to him, 'I am the way, the truth, and the life. No one comes to the Father except through Me.'" (John 14:6, NKJV).

Contrary to what almost every other world religion teaches, there is only one way to God, and that way is through Jesus! This is one distinction Christianity has from most other religions.

In 1971, I had been a Christian for one year, and I told everyone about Jesus. An acquaintance I had on the McConnell Air Force Base in Wichita, Kansas got tired of me asking him to go to church with me, so he told me he would go with me the next Sunday if I would go to a meeting regarding the Baha'i faith that Wednesday night—so I went.

Not realizing I had on a T-shirt which quoted John 14:6, I sat on the floor in the front row at this meeting. The teacher was making many emphatic claims, as though they were all true, but I did not know the Bible well enough to know if they were right or not. However, he finally made a claim that "even Jesus did not declare He was the only way to God." As soon as this Baha'i teacher said that, his eyes focused in on my shirt. He paused, and read it.

"I didn't know the Bible said that," he tried to backpedal. "I was always taught that Jesus said just the opposite," he went on.

"It sounds to me," I concluded, "that you've been taught a lot of wrong things."

The meeting was virtually over at that point, and I am proud to say that there were no converts to Baha'i that night, as far as I could tell.

Just like there is only one way to reach God—through Jesus—there is only one written revelation of God, which is His Word. His holy Scriptures—the Bible—are eternal.

> "Heaven and earth shall pass away, but My words shall not pass away." (Matthew 24:35, KJV).

Worshiping God any other way than through Jesus—and worshiping God any other way other than how He has revealed to us in the Bible—is not legitimate and is not "biblical worship."

Worship Is the Expression of Our Hearts

The word *worship* is, first of all, a verb of action. When used as a noun, it is referring to the acts of worship performed by a worshiper. Unless the worshiper is acting out of habit or tradition—where there is no real heart motive being acted upon—the actions of worship will always reflect the heart of the worshiper.

A heart attitude is never complete until it has been expressed. Perhaps you have heard the saying, "Love isn't love till it's given away." Love for Jesus is never complete until it is expressed. It is the expression of our love to God that we call worship.

We express our hearts to God with worship. We express our hearts to other beings in any way except worship. Worship is reserved for expressing our hearts to God only. Using worship to express our hearts to anyone or anything else other than God is wrong and very dangerous.

> "He who sacrifices to any god, except to the Lord only, he shall be utterly destroyed." (Exodus 22:20, NKJV).

Christian Worship Is Based on Love

Christianity and Judaism are the only religions in the world where worship is based on a love relationship with a deity. In all other world religions, worship is based on an unhealthy fear relationship with the object(s) of worship.

In many world religions, worship consists of the act or acts performed by *worshipers*, who are motivated by a need to appease a god or group of gods. If the worshipers do certain things, the god(s) will maybe not punish them or even somewhat reward them. Consequently, people who follow these religions never know when their god has been appeased or when their acts of worship have found them favor in their god's eyes. Therefore, these religions are perpetuated by fear—never love.

Christianity, which was born out of Judaism, is on the totally opposite end of the spectrum from these fear-based world religions. Let's do a short, simple comparison between most world religions and the relationship we have with Jesus, which is called Christianity.

World Religions/Christianity Comparison

Other World Religions	Christianity
The "worshiper" must do things to be accepted by their god(s)	Jesus already did all that needs to be done to purchase our redemption back to Himself, and we are accepted in the beloved (*Ephesians 1:6*).
Worship is based on what the "worshiper" can do for the deity.	Christian worship is based on what God, through Jesus, has already done for us (*Ephesians 1:7*).
The "worshiper" must do things to appease or please the object of their worship for fear of retaliation.	Our God would never retaliate against those whose worship was not done correctly; out of love, He simply corrects the worshiper for wrong worship. We see this in the story of Cain (*Genesis 4*).

Table 4

Worship and Blood Sacrifices

The worship of the almighty God has always been by blood. As a matter of fact, there can be no biblical worship without the shedding of innocent blood.

In the garden of Eden, God killed an animal so its skin could cover Adam and Eve's sin and shame. God instructed Moses that animal sacrifices must be made regularly to cover the sins of God's people. Sin is unholy, and it is the only thing which keeps mankind from being able to worship God.

> "For when Moses had spoken every precept to all the people according to the law, he took the blood of calves and goats, with water, scarlet wool, and hyssop, and sprinkled both the book itself and all the people, saying, "This is the blood of the covenant which God has commanded you." likewise he

sprinkled with blood both the tabernacle and all the vessels of the ministry. And according to the law almost all things are purified with blood, and without shedding of blood there is no remission (of sin)." (Hebrews 9:19–22, NKJV).

Now, in the new covenant, we can only access God to worship Him through Jesus, God's perfect lamb, whose blood was shed—not only to cover our sins, like the old covenant sacrifices did, but also to take our sins completely away.

"The next day John saw Jesus coming toward him, and said, 'Behold! The Lamb of God who takes away the sin of the world!'" (John 1:29, NKJV)

This is how God made a way for us to enter into a loving relationship with Him so we can express that love to Him through worship. Do you remember chapter one of this book? We studied what God is doing in the earth. Isaiah 61:11 told us that God is establishing righteousness and praise before all the nations of the earth. It is impossible to biblically praise God without righteousness being established first. Without a relationship with a holy God, which is achieved by allowing Him to make us holy with His blood, there is no relationship with God through which we can express our love to God. Again, you cannot express praise and worship to God without His blood being applied to your life. The old revival song of the early 1900s said it best:

> Are you washed in the blood
> In the soul-cleansing blood of the Lamb?
> Are your garments spotless? Are they white as snow?
> Are they washed in the blood of the Lamb?

Although Cain did not understand the depth of the meanings of blood sacrifice associated with all worship of the true and living God, we simply must assume from the story of Cain that God had made it clear to Cain and Abel how He wanted to be worshiped. Even if it was not clear to Cain how God wanted to be worshiped by the shedding of blood at first, when God received Abel's worship and rejected Cain's offering, that should have made it clear to Cain. Cain would have understood this if he had been listening or paying attention to God. Instead, Cain was wrapped up in himself. Cain was self-absorbed, self-centered, and self-pleasing—not God-centered or God-pleasing.

The Story of Cain

It is very important that we take the time to read the story of Cain so we can understand how God reacts to people who do not worship Him the way He desires to be worshiped.

> "Now Abel kept flocks, and Cain worked the soil. In the course of time Cain brought some of the fruits of the soil as an offering (of worship) to the LORD. But Abel brought fat portions from some of the firstborn of his flock. The LORD looked with favor on Abel and his offering (of worship), but on Cain and his offering he did not look with favor. So Cain was very angry, and his face was downcast. Then the LORD said to Cain, "Why are you angry? Why is your face downcast? If you do what is right, will you not be accepted?" (Genesis 4:2–7, NIV).

Cain's worship was self-willed and self-centered. Cain worked the ground to produce crops for food. Therefore, he wanted to bring an offering to God based on his own works, not what God required. Cain's worship was based on what would make Cain feel good, not what God asked of him.

We see this same attitude in our present-day offerings of worship as well. Musicians—whose life is their music, not Jesus—care more about the excellence of their musical offerings than the state of their hearts as they play their music.

Here is the revelation King David, the musician, received from God on this issue when approaching and worshiping God.

> "Create in me a clean heart, O God; and renew a right spirit within me. Cast me not away from thy presence; and take not thy holy spirit from me. Restore unto me the joy of thy salvation; and uphold me with thy free spirit. Then will I teach transgressors thy ways; and sinners shall be converted

unto thee. Deliver me from **blood** guiltiness, O God, thou God of my salvation: and my tongue shall sing aloud of thy **righteousness**. O Lord, open thou my lips; and my mouth shall shew forth thy **praise**. For thou desirest not sacrifice; else would I give it: thou delightest not in burnt offering. The sacrifices of God are a broken spirit: a broken and a contrite heart, O God, thou wilt not despise." (Psalm 51:10–17, KJV).

Notice in this Scripture that the most important thing to David is the presence of God, which only comes to someone who has a clean heart before God. Out of this right spirit is birthed music *from* God, which we give back to Him as our offering of praise.

Cain's worship reminds me of a little child who has colored a picture and wants to show off his handiwork. "Look, God; look what grew when I planted seeds in the ground."

Whereas mommy and daddy will tell their child how good the picture they colored is—even when it is not great compared to the skills of other children—they will seldom compromise the truth on matters of importance, such as brushing the teeth or taking a bath regularly. That's because mommy and daddy know something about the health risks when those things are not done.

Likewise, Jesus knows the spiritual health risks when we engage in self-willed and self-centered worship. Therefore, He will not compromise the truth concerning worship, and He will not tell us we are doing well when we are not. God spoke to Cain and said,

"If you do what is right, will you not be accepted?" (Genesis 4:7, NIV)

Notice God was not angry at Cain's self-willed worship. God simply encouraged Cain to worship correctly so his worship could be accepted, like his brother's worship. A parent seldom gets angry at his or her child when the child tries to brush his or her teeth properly, even though the child has not mastered the entire technique yet. But these parents will still not compromise the correct way to brush teeth, no matter how long it takes the child to learn it. They will painstakingly explain—over and over—how to brush teeth until the child catches on.

This is like God's attitude toward His children while they are learning the importance of worshiping Him correctly. God has an infinite amount of patience with His children while we are learning how to worship Him. On the other hand, we humans will run out of patience with our children the second we suspect they are not trying. We must be careful to never assume that God treats us the way most of us treat our children. God's grace and mercy allow Him to be patient with us, even when we intentionally do not do things His way, like Cain. However, His patience should never be interpreted as compromising the truth of how He wants to be worshiped.

Self-Willed Worship vs. Biblical Worship

In the story of Cain and Abel, we see a fundamentally different attitude between these two brothers concerning their responsibilities.

> "Now Abel kept flocks, and Cain worked the soil." (Genesis 4:2, NIV).

Cain *worked,* but Abel *kept.* Stewardship, not ownership, is the correct attitude of a worshiper. By that, I mean worship is *not* to be the fruit of our own labor. Worship is to be the acknowledgment and giving of thanks to God for the fruit of His labor and abundant provision for us.

Cain "worked the soil," but Abel "kept flocks." The ground was cursed by God (Genesis 3:17); therefore, its fruit could never please God. Blood, on the other hand, represents the cost of true worship—death to self, and the purchase price it cost God to redeem mankind back to Himself.

The sacrificial lamb became the symbol of God coming to earth in the flesh throughout the entire Bible, which means Abel's offering foreshadowed the coming of Jesus, whose blood and death paid for our sins.

The "Way" of Cain

Cain refused to worship God the way God required—with a blood sacrifice—so his offering was not accepted by God. Even before he made his offering to God, Cain could have traded grain for a lamb with his brother. After God refused Cain's worship expression of grain, Cain could have purchased a lamb from his brother, and his offering would have been accepted by God just as much as Abel's offering was.

This was not meant to be such a big deal. Worship God His way, and the worship will be accepted. Don't worship God His way, and your worship won't be accepted. That's all Cain had to worry about. That's like the parent who says, "Brush your teeth this way, and you will get your teeth clean. Brush your teeth other ways, and your teeth will not get as clean as they should be."

But Cain refused to go to the effort of doing things God's way—even when he was given more than one chance to accomplish that task with no fear of God retaliating against him for not doing things right. This is what the Bible calls "the way of Cain." It could be summed up this way: immaturity plus being unteachable results in self-gratifying worship of God. This is a deadly combination, as Cain found out.

The Three Deadly Sins of the Last Days According to Jude

Jude is a very powerful, yet short one-chapter book in the Bible that has one overall theme. That theme is announced in Jude verse 4.

> "For certain men have crept in unnoticed, who long ago were
> marked out for this condemnation, ungodly men, who turn
> the grace of our God into lewdness and deny the only Lord
> God and our Lord Jesus Christ." (Jude 4, NKJV).

Although Jude touches on other topics in his short book, most of the chapter deals with this subject of "ungodly men" who have crept into the church. His warning is clearly identified to the church which is living "in the last time."

> "But you, beloved, remember the words which were spoken
> before by the apostles of our Lord Jesus Christ: how they told you
> that there would be mockers in the last time who would walk
> according to their own ungodly lusts." (Jude 17-18, NKJV).

These ungodly men found in the church in the last days will be recognized by three distinct sins.

> "*Woe unto them! for they have gone in the way of Cain, and ran greedily after the error of Balaam for reward, and perished in the gainsaying of Core.*" (Jude 11, KJV)

Let's take just a few moments to outline these three most serious sins before we proceed in our study of worship.

The Prominent Sins of the Last-Days Church

The way of Cain	Genesis 4:1–8	Self-centered worship
The error of Balaam	Numbers 22–24	Making money from your spiritual gift
The gainsaying of Core	Numbers 16	Rebelling at God's appointed authority

Table 5

These are the three sins which these ungodly men will be known for in the last-days church, according to Jude. Look with me at the sins of each of these men Jude has named.

The sin of Cain is said to be his way. If a person is a certain way, it implies he or she is set in that way and has no intentions of changing. We call that being unteachable. The way someone is we first attribute to his or her attitude. If the attitude is never adjusted, this way is attributed to the person's personality (i.e., "That's the way she is.").

The sin of Balaam is an error or a mistake. One seemingly innocent mistake nearly cost Balaam his life; however, his donkey protected him. Sure, we all make mistakes, but the mistake Balaam made is the result of a character flaw—one which Balaam should have known better than to make as a prophet of God. We can never fudge on God's principles.

The sin of Core is gainsaying. This is an old English term which is not in use anymore. We would use the term *rebellion* instead. Yet that does not explain the attitude growing to personality implied by the word *gainsaying*. It too refers to the way someone is; yet it is specifically related to authority. In other words, someone who is gainsaying is one who always disagrees with the established authority. The gainsayer does not disagree with the leader based on principle, but always takes the opposite side of the one in authority and stirs up others to rebel, as well. Let's look at the results of these three sins.

The Outcome or Consequences of These Sins

The Sins	Outcome or Consequences
The way of Cain	Cain's sin caused him to murder his brother, whose worship was accepted by God, and to endure the consequences of that action for the rest of his life.
The error of Balaam	God would have killed Balaam if his donkey had not spoken up to warn him. His ministry was capped, and he never reached his full potential in God after that.
The gainsaying of Core	Core (Kora) and his two friends, along with their entire households—which included their children's families, their flocks and herds, and all that they owned along with their servants and their servant's families—were swallowed by the earth, which opened up and closed back up over them. The 250 men they had influenced against Moses were burnt to ashes when fire came down from heaven at the same time the earth was swallowing the three leaders.

Table 6

These Sins in the Church Today

These three sins are currently very prominent in the church in this current period of history. This is yet another confirmation that we are approaching the time of Jesus' return.

God was angry at Core and his friends, and God was angry at Balaam. But God was not angry with Cain—at first. If God had been angry in this situation with Cain, He would have punished Cain for worshiping wrong—but He didn't punish Cain. Cain reacted like most immature Christians do when their worship is not accepted by God. Cain got mad at the one whose worship was accepted by God, and Cain got mad at God for not accepting his worship. However, Cain could not strike out against God, so he attacked the person whose worship had been accepted by God. We see that same response in the church today. Those who have not yet discovered how to enter into the presence of God through worship often criticize those who have discovered this.

Just like Balaam, the church today is full of people who sell their gifts for rewards. Try booking a Christian recording artist or a published worship leader in your church. You will find out very quickly who has fallen for the same error of Balaam. This error is rampant throughout the entire church, as well. Some do not sell their gifts for money, but for recognition or position. If they lose these or are not given them, they cease to offer their spiritual gifts, calling, or talent and show themselves to have no real personal worship relationship with Christ when they walk in this error.

Core's sin of rebellion is active throughout the church today, as well. It is the norm to leave a church when you disagree with the leadership and to stir up everybody you can against the church leadership in the process. This is exactly what Core did, and God still thinks the same about that sort of sin. God will punish this sin with the same severity sooner or later. Don't think that just because your world has not swallowed you up yet, you are exempt. This is simply a grace period from God giving you time to repent.

Let us search our hearts and purge ourselves of these and other sins! Let us, like King David, pursue the presence of our God from a broken spirit—then we will start to understand God's command for us to worship Him in the beauty of holiness.

> "Give unto the LORD the glory due unto His name; worship the LORD in the beauty of holiness." (Psalm 29:2, KJV).

> "Ascribe to the LORD the glory due His name; worship the LORD in the splendor of His holiness." (Psalm 29:2, NIV).

> "Give unto the Lord the glory due to His name; Worship the Lord in the beauty of holiness." (Psalm 29:2, NKJV).

Chapter Three

Biblical Synonyms for Worship

Worship Is a General Term with Many Synonyms

To Christians, to worship means to express our love to God in ways that God has asked or commanded us. The Bible uses many different words to describe the act of worship. For instance, in this Scripture, we can find three different synonyms for the word *worship*.

> "I will bless the LORD at all times: His praise shall continually be in my mouth. My soul shall make her **boast** in the LORD: the humble shall hear thereof, and be glad." (Psalm 34:1–2).

The first synonym mentioned in this Scripture is *bless*. To bless someone is to show him or her much honor, respect, or praise. It is to lift that person up in such a way that he or she is personally blessed to have you around them. To bless the Lord is to worship the Lord.

The second synonym mentioned here is *praise*. To bless the Lord is to praise the Lord, which is the same thing as worshiping the Lord. Generally speaking, these words all refer to the expression of our love to almighty God.

The third synonym for the biblical word *worship* is *boast*. Notice who the object of our boasting is in this Scripture: *"to the Lord."* Therefore, to boast to the Lord is the same thing as blessing the Lord, which is the same thing as praising the Lord, which is the same as worshiping the

Lord. In the general sense, these are all biblical synonyms of each other which basically have the same meaning.

The list of words which the Bible uses as synonyms to the word *worship* grows on and on: *glorify, magnify, exalt,* and *serve* are just a few more of these many synonyms. Perhaps several other of these synonyms are coming to mind right now. Take a minute to write them down so you can look them up in the Bible later.

The Difference between Synonyms and Expressions

Please do not mistake the synonyms of the word *worship* for the actual expressions of worship.

For instance, one way we can express worship to God is by kneeling before the Lord. Kneeling, then, is a physical worship expression of the heart's feeling of love toward God. Kneeling, in this case, becomes the expression of worship directed toward God. Worship becomes the result of this physical expression when it comes out of a feeling of love toward God.

Just because kneeling can be a physical expression of worship or adoration of God, it does not mean that every time we kneel, it is an act of worship to God. Sometimes we kneel to find out what is under the bed. That action is not worship. Sometimes we kneel to propose marriage, but that action of kneeling is still not worship. Expressing love through worship is reserved for showing our love to almighty God only, not other humans or any other spiritual beings.

What makes an action worship is the condition of the person's heart, mind, and emotions when the action is performed.

Clapping can be a physical expression of praise and worship to God. However, not every time we clap are we worshiping God. Sometimes we clap to show appreciation to someone. Other times, we clap to scare off a cat. What makes clapping an act of worship is the heart, mind, and emotions of the person clapping.

A worship expression is a physical act directed toward God to honor and bless God. Other expressions of worship can include singing, shouting, leaping, bowing, and lifting the hands. We will cover these worship expressions more extensively in the book entitled *Portrait of a Worshiper.*

In conclusion, worship occurs when what is in the heart, mind, and emotions of a worshiper is *physically expressed* in some way to God.

Some Biblical Synonyms for Worship

Here is an introductory list of biblical synonyms of the general term *worship* and the Bible reference where they are found. For most of these, you will find many more Scripture references where these synonyms are used in the Bible. It could be interesting to use a certain color of highlighter to mark every synonym of the word *worship* that you come across in your Bible.

Take the time to read each of these Scriptures listed here for yourself to verify that each word is used as a synonym of the word *worship*. This is not meant to be an exhaustive list of synonyms, but an introductory list whereby you are able to understand the concept. This list is in no particular order.

Biblical Synonyms for Worship

Thanksgiving	Psalm 116:17 KJV
Exalt	Isaiah 25:1 KJV
Honor	John 5:23 KJV
Adore	Psalm 149:6 LB
Glorify	Psalm 22:23 KJV
Bless	Psalm 145:2 KJV
Extol	Psalm 30:1 KJV
Exult	Psalm 68:3 LB
Praise	Psalm 150:6 KJV
Laud	Romans 15:11 KJV
Shine	Isaiah 60:1 KJV
Worship	John 4:23 KJV
Magnify	Luke 1:46 KJV
Rejoice	Philippians 4:4 KJV

Table 7

Chapter Four

Defining Biblical Worship

Why Learn Definitions?

Every time any subject is approached by a teacher, that teacher does well to define the terms used to teach. This insures fewer misunderstandings resulting from different definitions of the same words. For instance, if I use the word *worship*, some may think that I mean "slower songs done in church right before the sermon." But that is not what I am referring to at all when I use the word *worship*. Therefore, it is very important to define the terms we will be using in the Worship College text books to eliminate as many misunderstandings as possible.

However, rather than tell you personality-based definitions of biblical words translated into the synonyms of *worship*, I believe we should find out the definitions for these words from respected theologians and scholars.

The Bible was written mostly in two languages—Hebrew and Greek. Therefore, it is important for us to understand the original languages of the Bible when doing biblical word studies. This, then, must be an important part of our starting place for understanding biblical worship. This is so, when we talk about worship, we will think of the same things.

Important Information for This Chapter

The definitions shared in this chapter are from *Strong's Concordance* and/or *Vine's Bible Dictionary*, unless otherwise indicated.

This chapter is not an exhaustive study of biblical words translated into the synonyms of the word *worship*. It is, rather, only an introduction to these various definitions. It is also an example of how every person can use these common study tools to discover "revelation knowledge," and truth for themselves.

Revelation knowledge is, first of all, spiritual knowledge which is revealed to us by the Holy Spirit of God through the Word of God—the Bible. In this case, however, the Holy Spirit has used these common Bible study tools to reveal further truths about worship.

From the first Greek word mentioned in this chapter to the end of the chapter, the information you will find within boxes will be my thoughts and commentary. Everything else in the outline form, has been taken straight out of these resource books, and is reprinted here for your convenience only. Please understand that this material is copyrighted and is reprinted by permission.

We will begin by discussing several Greek words found in the Bible which have been translated into some of the synonyms of the word "Worship."

Greek Words

Proskuneo

1. This is the most frequent Greek word rendered "to worship" in the Bible
   a) Strong's Greek Number 4352
      i) Greek word: proskuneo pros-koo-neh'-o
      ii) Part of Speech: verb

> A verb is an action or state of being. Worship is an action—an expression of an attitude of the heart.

    iii) Vine's Word(s): Worship, Worshiping

b) Usage Notes: KJV Total Count: 60—it is the most frequent word rendered "to worship."

    i) (from pros, "towards," and kuneo, "to **kiss**") to kiss the hand to (towards) one, in token of reverence

> Worship is an intimate expression of deep love and appreciation for Jehovah God.

    ii) Among the Orientals, esp. the Persians, to fall upon the knees and touch the ground with the forehead as an expression of profound reverence

> Worship is expressed from humility before almighty God, not pride.

    iii) in the NT by kneeling or prostration to do homage (to one) or make obeisance, whether in order to express respect or to make supplication

> Supplication is "humble prayer" to a deity. Prayer, then, is an expression of Worship.

    iv) "to make obeisance, do reverence to"
       a) **o·bei·sance** (o-bâ¹sens, o-bê¹-) noun[1]
          (1) A gesture or movement of the body, such as a curtsy, that expresses deference or homage.
          (2) An attitude of deference or homage.
          (3) [*Middle English obeisaunce, from Old French obeissance, from obeissant, present participle of obeir, to obey. See OBEY.*]

---

1   *The American Heritage® Dictionary of the English Language, Third Edition*

> To worship is to obey God, who has both commanded us to worship Him and commanded us as to how we are to worship Him.

(4) — o·bei·sant *adjective*

c) In the Bible, proskuneo is used as an act of homage or reverence which is directed in six different directions

    i) **to God**–*"then saith Jesus unto him, Get thee hence, Satan: for it is written, Thou shalt worship the Lord thy God, and him only shalt thou* **serve**.*" (Matt 4:10, KJV)*

> Notice that worship of the Lord is the same thing as serving the Lord. There is no other way to serve God directly than to worship Him. We serve God; we minister to other people. Serving God is worship. Ministry is serving mankind.

    ii) **to Christ**–*"And, behold, there came a leper and worshiped him, saying, Lord, if thou wilt, thou canst make me clean." (Matt 8:2, KJV)*

    iii) **to a man**–*"The servant therefore fell down, and worshiped him, saying, Lord, have patience with me, and I will pay thee all." (Matt 18:26, KJV)*

> This is the only reference to someone worshiping a man in Scripture. This is not a true story, but a parable told by Jesus in which the one being worshiped is a type of God or Christ.

    iv) **to the Dragon,** by men, **to the Beast**–*"And they worshiped the dragon which gave power unto the beast: and they worshiped the beast, saying, who is like unto the beast? who is able to make war with him? (Rev 13:4, KJV)*

    v) **to demons and to idols**–*"And the rest of the men which were not killed by these plagues yet repented not of the works of their hands, that they* **should not worship** *devils, and idols of gold, and silver, and brass, and stone, and of wood: which neither can see, nor hear, nor walk: (Rev 9:20, KJV)*

> Worship of the dragon or the beast, demons, and idols are clearly identified as wrong or false worship. Those who worship these are clearly identified as those who worship from deception, not truth.

> **vi)** **to angels**—*"And I John saw these things, and heard them. And when I had heard and seen, I fell down to worship before the feet of the angel which shewed me these things. Then saith he unto me, see thou do it not: for I am thy fellowservant, and of thy brethren the prophets, and of them which keep the sayings of this book:* **worship God.***" (Rev 22:8-9, KJV)*

> This is the only biblical reference of a man worshiping an angel. When the man tried to worship the angel, he was quickly corrected and told God is the only one who should receive worship.
>
> Upon careful examination of all these objects of worship mentioned above, we can simply conclude that our Lord and God should be the only recipient of our worship according to the Bible.

Other Greek Words

2. Other Greek words translated "Worship"
   a) Greek Word: **sebomai**
      i) Part of Speech: Verb
      ii) Strong's Number: 4576
      iii) Usage Notes: "to revere," stressing the feeling of awe or devotion

> True worship comes from a sense of awe regarding almighty God.

   b) Greek Word: **sebazomai**
      i) Part of Speech: Verb
      ii) Strong's Number: 4573
      iii) Usage Notes: akin to 4576, "to honor religiously,"

> To honor religiously means to make a commitment to become a worshiper, no matter the cost.

c) Greek Word: **latreuo**
   i) Part of Speech: Verb
   ii) Strong's Number: 3000
   iii) Usage Notes: "to serve, to render religious service or homage," is translated "to worship" in Phil. 3:3, "(who) worship (by the Spirit of God)," RV, AV, "(which) worship (God in the spirit);" the RV renders it "to serve" (for AV, "to worship") in Acts 7:42; Acts 24:14; AV and RV, "(the) worshipers" in Heb. 10:2, present participle, lit., "(the ones) worshiping." See SERVE.

> Ministry is serving mankind or a church. Worship is serving God.

d) Greek Word: **eusebeo**
   i) Part of Speech: Verb
   ii) Strong's Number: 2151
   iii) Usage Notes: "to act piously towards," is translated "ye worship" in Acts 17:23. See PIETY (to show).

> "O worship the LORD in the beauty of holiness." (Psalm 96:9, NKJV).

e) Greek Word: **sebasma**
   i) Part of Speech: Noun
   ii) Strong's Number: 4574
   iii) Usage Notes: denotes "an object of worship" (akin to 4573); Acts 17:23 (see DEVOTION);in 2Thess. 2:4, "that is worshiped;" every object of "worship," whether the true God or pagan idols, will come under the ban of the Man of Sin.

> "He that sacrificeth unto any god, save unto the LORD only, he shall be utterly destroyed." (Exodus 22:20, KJV).

f) Greek Word: **ethelothreskeia[-ia]**
   i) Part of Speech: Noun
   ii) Strong's Number: 1479
   iii) Usage Notes: "will-worship" (ethelo, "to **will**," threskeia, "worship"), occurs in Col. 2:23, voluntarily adopted "worship," whether unbidden or forbidden, not that which is imposed by others, but which one affects.

> "We will go into His tabernacles: we will worship at His footstool." (Psalm 132:7, KJV).

> To be a worshiper requires a resolute decision, or an irrevocable commitment!

g) Greek Word: **threskeia**
   i) Part of Speech: Noun
   ii) Strong's Number: 2356
   iii) Usage Notes: for which see RELIGION, is translated "worshiping" in Col. 2:18.
   Note: In Luke 14:10, AV, doxa, "glory" (RV), is translated "worship."

Hebrew Words

Halal

1. **"Halal"** – a Hebrew word for "Praise"
   h) Strong's Hebrew Number 1984
      i) Hebrew word: halal haw-lal'
      ii) Part of Speech: verb
      iii) Root: a primitive root
      iv) Found more than 160 times in the Old Testament

i) An excerpt from the Vine's article – "The word halal is the source of "Hallelujah," a Hebrew expression of "praise" to God which has been taken over into virtually every language of mankind. The Hebrew "Hallelujah" is generally translated "Praise the Lord!" The Hebrew term is more technically translated "Let us praise Yah," the term "Yah" being a shortened form of "Yahweh," the unique Israelite name for God. ... The Greek approximation of "Hallelujah" is found 4 times in the New Testament in the form "Alleluia".

j) Meanings of "halal"
    i) **to shine / to give light**
        a) to shine (fig. of God's favor)
        b) to flash forth light

In chapter one of this book I told you about going shopping for my wife's diamond engagement ring. The jeweler placed a black cloth on top of the glass counter directly under a spot light. There was no light within the diamonds themselves. They could only reflect and refract the brilliance of the light above them.

When we worship God, we do not shine on our own; rather, we simply reflect the favor and the glory of God in the way the moon reflects the glory of the sun, or a diamond flashes with light at the moment it becomes properly aligned with a light source, and the eye of the beholder.

God's "black cloth" is the darkness of sin in the world. Against it, a true worshiper who has positioned himself or herself to reflect the glory of God will flash forth God's glory in the earth in a greater way than when he or she is set against the "glass countertop" of our churches. A true worshiper worships everywhere, not just in church.

---

    ii) **to be clear (of sound or color)**

To be **clear of sound** in relationship to worshiping and praising God implies to us the importance of having a "clear sound of worship" in our corporate worship gatherings. Poorly mixed sound will destroy the anointing of the presence of God! We have to be careful here that we do not superimpose our personal tastes in music, and think that is what is needed to have a "clear sound." Music style is not the issue here, the audible clarity of the music is the issue.

"And even things without life giving sound, whether pipe or harp, except they give a distinction in the sounds, how shall it be known what is piped or harped? For if the trumpet give an uncertain sound, who shall prepare himself to the battle? So likewise ye, except ye utter by the tongue words easy to be understood, how shall it be known what is spoken? for ye shall speak into the air. There are, it may be, so many kinds of voices in the world, and none of them is without signification. Therefore if I know not the meaning of the voice, I shall be unto him that speaketh a barbarian, and he that speaketh shall be a barbarian unto me." (1 Corinthians 14:7–11, KJV).

To be **clear of color** in relationship to worship can refer to visual artistic stimuli in the place of corporate worship, such as stained glass; banners; interior decoration; worship props, such as streamers, ribbons, or flags; as well as worship attire. Even the secular world understands the influence of color upon the human subconscious mind and emotions and how different colors influence us in different ways. I believe color can have a similar effect upon the human spirit as well. In the only account in the Bible where God is quoted in detail as to how He wanted His place of worship to look, color was a vital part of the design.

"And this is the offering which ye shall take of them (for the tabernacle); gold, and silver, and brass, And blue, and purple, and scarlet, and fine linen, and goats' hair, And rams' skins dyed red, and badgers' skins, and shittim wood, Oil for the light, spices for anointing oil, and for sweet incense, Onyx stones, and stones to be set in the ephod, and in the breastplate. And let them make me a sanctuary; that I may dwell among them. According to all that I show thee, after the pattern of the tabernacle, and the pattern of all the instruments thereof, even so shall ye make it." (Exodus 25:3–9, KJV).

"Moreover thou shalt make the tabernacle with ten curtains of fine twined linen, and blue, and purple, and scarlet: with cherubim of cunning work shalt thou make them." (Exodus 26:1, KJV).

We perceive both sound and color (which is revealed in light) as part of the electromagnetic spectrum. This spectrum is made up of vibrations vibrating at different frequencies. It progresses from sound waves to light waves, the faster the frequencies of the vibrations. Between the vibrations we can hear and see are other useful vibration frequencies such as radio waves, microwaves, x-rays, and gamma rays.

Our human brain can receive and process vibrations through our ears on the average of between 20 to 20,000 vibrations per second. The more frequent the vibrations, the higher the perceived "pitch" or "note" the sound vibrations make.

Radio waves are vibrations which are transmitted at frequencies higher than the human ear can receive and process. Therefore these vibrations are beyond our human audible range. What makes these radio waves useful to us is if we have a receiver which can re-modulate the radio frequencies into frequencies which our human ears can hear.

Light, on the other hand, are frequencies most of which are able to be received and processed through our eyes. However, there are certain frequencies of light which we cannot see with our naked eye. X-rays and gamma rays, for instance, cannot be seen with the human eye, but when used in conjunction with the right modulating equipment, can be very useful within the medical and security fields.

At sea level, sound travels at approximately 770 mph. Light, on the other hand, travels at approximately 670,616,700 mph. Isn't it amazing how God created us to receive and process such a wide range of vibration frequencies? Worship must be clear on both ends of the electromagnetic spectrum, if it is to fulfill this definition of "halal."

iii) to sing (praises)

Because music and singing are so important to corporate worship, they are synonymous with praise and worship in the Bible. *"Serve the LORD with gladness: come before His presence with singing."* (Psalm 100:2, KJV).

iv) to celebrate

The only One we are to celebrate is Jesus, our Creator and God. He is the celebrated one—the only one we are to make a "celebrity."

v) to make a show

There are two ways of understanding this phrase. First, because praise and worship is associated with the arts—especially performing arts, like music and dance—there is a correlation between praise and the excellence of the expression of our praise. *"Sing forth the honour of His name: make His praise glorious."* (Psalm 66:2, KJV).

Secondly, this phrase could be paraphrased "to appear as a show-off while expressing praise." *"But ye are a chosen generation, a royal priesthood, an holy nation, a peculiar people; that ye should shew forth the praises of Him who hath called you out of darkness into His marvelous light."* (1 Peter 2:9, KJV).

vi) to boast, praise , be boastful
   a) to be boastful, boastful ones, boasters (participle)
   b) to praise, boast, make a boast
   c) to boast, glory, make one's boast

"My God's better than your God," the Buddhist said to the Christian missionary.

"Really?" the Christian responded. "Why don't we just compare our gods, then? You go first."

"All right," the Buddhist accepted. "Buddha was born for the sole purpose of bringing enlightenment to his people."

"Interesting," the Christian thought out loud. "So was Jesus."

"Buddha lived a life of example for his people and taught them great wisdom," the Buddhist continued.

"Is that so?" the Christian blurted out. "Well, Jesus did that too!"

"Buddha gave his whole life and even died for the sake of his people."

"My, my," the Christian smirked, "Jesus did that as well."

There was an awkward pause as the Christian leaned in toward the Buddhist, turning the palms of his hands up, waiting a few seconds, and gesturing again, saying, "Go on!"

"What do you mean, 'Go on'?" The Buddhist looked puzzled.

"Well, Jesus rose from the dead!" the Christian exclaimed energetically.

Hanging his head, the Buddhist confessed, "Well, Buddha hasn't made it yet."

vii) **to commend**, to be praised, be made praiseworthy, be commended, be worthy of praise

Here is how Isaiah commended the Lord "O LORD, thou art my God; I will exalt thee, I will praise Thy name; for Thou hast done wonderful things; Thy counsels of old are faithfulness and truth." (Isaiah 25:1, KJV).

viii)　　**to rave**

Here is a biblical example of someone raving:

Then the Levites, Jeshua, and Kadmiel, Bani, Hashabniah, Sherebiah, Hodijah, Shebaniah, and Pethahiah, said, Stand up and bless the LORD your God forever and ever: and blessed be Thy glorious name, which is exalted above all blessing and praise. Thou, even Thou, art LORD alone; Thou hast made heaven, the heaven of heavens, with all their host, the earth, and all things that are therein, the seas, and all that is therein, and Thou preservest them all; and the host of heaven worshipeth Thee. Thou art the LORD the God, Who didst choose Abram, and broughtest him forth out of Ur of the Chaldees, and gavest him the name of Abraham; And foundest his heart faithful before Thee, and madest a covenant with him to give the land of the Canaanites, the Hittites, the Amorites, and the Perizzites, and the Jebusites, and the Girgashites, to give it, I say, to his seed, and hast performed Thy words; for Thou art righteous: And didst see the affliction of our fathers in Egypt, and heardest their cry by the Red sea; And shewedst signs and wonders upon Pharaoh, and on all his servants, and on all the people of his land: for thou knewest that they dealt proudly against them. So didst Thou get Thee a name, as it is this day. And Thou didst divide the sea before them, so that they went through the midst of the sea on the dry land; and their persecutors Thou threwest into the deeps, as a stone into the mighty waters. Moreover Thou leddest them in the day by a cloudy pillar; and in the night by a pillar of fire, to give them light in the way wherein they should go. Thou camest down also upon mount Sinai, and spakest with them from heaven, and gavest them right judgments, and true laws, good statutes and commandments: And madest known unto them Thy holy sabbath, and commandedst them precepts, statutes, and laws, by the hand of Moses Thy servant: And gavest them bread from heaven for their hunger, and broughtest forth water for them out of the rock for their thirst, and promisedst them that they should go in to possess the land which Thou hadst sworn to give them." (Nehemiah 9:5–15, KJV).

Have you ever noticed that when someone raves about something or someone, they just go on and on about what they are so excited about? One aspect of raving in our worship is to be so focused on the object of our worship that we even lose track of time as we are raving about who He is and what He has done.

ix) **to rage**

> "And when the chief priests and scribes saw the wonderful things that He did, and the children crying in the temple, and saying, Hosanna to the Son of David; they were sore displeased, And said unto Him, Hearest thou what these say? And Jesus saith unto them, Yea; have ye never read, Out of the mouth of babes and sucklings Thou hast perfected praise?" (Matthew 21:15–16, KJV)

If you've ever seen children get excited about something, then you know the definition of rage. It is noteworthy that Jesus refers to this type of out-of-control crying out in worship as "perfected praise." In other words, this is where He wants us to get in our praise, which begs the question, "How far away from this goal are we at this stage of our own development in expressing worship to God?"

x) **to act madly,** act like a madman
xi) **to be clamorously foolish**
   a) to make a fool of,
   b) make into a fool
   c) **...while giving glory**

There can be no doubt as to God's intention concerning *halal* or praise where He is concerned. When mankind worships God, it is to be with such absolute reckless abandonment of our own consciousness and intense focus on Him that we appear clamorously foolish and crazy to the onlookers. Praise of our God is to be executed with total disregard for personal dignity, with 100 percent of our focus and energy toward Him. How far away from this standard have we digressed in our corporate church gatherings? We have even adapted various models of worship which condone the very opposite of this. We say we are trying to be sensitive to seekers; in actuality, we are using this excuse to create self-gratifying, comfortable, middle-of-the-road worship experiences which do not at all resemble how God has told us He wants to be praised.

k) Summary of translation and usage: In the King James Bible "halal" is translated into praise 117 times, glory 14 times, boast 10 times, mad 8 times, shine 3 times, foolish 3 times, fools 2 times, commended 2 times, rage 2 times, celebrate 1 time, give 1 time, marriage 1 time, and renowned 1 time for a Total Count of 165 times.

Other Hebrew Words

3. Other Old Testament words translated "Praise"
   a) Word: **yadah**

I'm told it was Jerry Seinfeld who popularized the use of the phrase "yada, yada" as a cool way to say "etc., etc." I wonder if he or his writers would have been so quick to use that word if they had known they were actually praising God every time they said it.

   i) Strong's Number: 3034
   ii) Part of Speech: verb
   iii) Usage Notes: "to give thanks, laud, praise." A common Hebrew word in all its periods, this verb is an important word in the language of worship. Yadah is found nearly 120

times in the Hebrew Bible, the first time being in the story of the birth of Judah, Jacob's son who was born to Leah: "*And she conceived again and bore a son, and said, This time I will praise the Lord; therefore she called his name Judah*" (Gen. 29:35, RSV).

The name Judah is a form of the word *yadah*.

---

iv) As is to be expected, this word is found most frequently in the Book of Psalms (some 70 times). As an expression of thanks or praise, it is a natural part of ritual or <u>public worship</u> as well as <u>personal praise</u> to God (Psa. 30:9, 12; Psa. 35:18).

Notice there is a distinction between public worship and personal praise according to these scholars. Herein lies the foundational premise for our studies on individual worship and corporate worship.

---

v) Thanks often are directed to the name of the Lord (Psa. 106:47; Psa. 122:4). The variation in translation may be seen in 1Kings 8:33: "confess" thy name (KJV, NEB, NASB); "acknowledge" (RSV); "praise" (JB, NAB).

b) Word: t(e)hillah

  i) Strong's Number: 8416

  ii) Part of Speech: Noun

  iii) Usage Notes: "glory; praise; song of praise; praiseworthy deeds." T(e)hillah occurs 57 times and in all periods of biblical Hebrew.

    a) First, this word denotes a quality or attribute of some person or thing, "glory or praiseworthiness": "*He is thy praise, and he is thy God, that hath done for thee these great and terrible things, which thine eyes have seen*" (Deut. 10:21, KJV). Israel is God's "glory" when she exists in a divinely exalted and blessed state: "*And give him no rest, till he*

establish, and till he make Jerusalem a praise in the earth"
(Isa. 62:7;KJV cf. Jer. 13:11).

He (God) is *our* t(e)hillah (praise). We are to be a praise (t[e]hillah) to Him.

---

b) Second, in some cases t(e)hillah represents the words or song by which God is publicly lauded, or by which His "glory" is publicly declared: "My *praise* [the Messiah is speaking here] *shall be of thee in the great congregation."* (Psa. 22:25a, KJV). Psa. 22:22, KJV is even clearer: "*I will declare thy name unto my brethren: in the midst of the congregation will I praise thee."*

T(e)hillah is the public declaration or song of praise to almighty God.

---

c) In a third nuance t(e)hillah is a technical-musical term for a song (sir) which exalts or praises God: "David's psalm of praise" (heading for Psa. 145:1 in the Hebrew). Perhaps Neh. 11:17 refers to a choirmaster or one who conducts such singing of "praises": "And Mattaniah ..., the son of Asaph, was the principal to begin the thanksgiving in prayer [who at the beginning was the leader of praise at prayer]...." Finally, t(e)hillah may represent deeds which are worthy of "praise," or deeds for which the doer deserves "praise and glory." This meaning is in the word's first biblical appearance: "*Who is like unto thee, O Lord, among the gods? Who is like thee, glorious in holiness, fearful in praises* [in praiseworthy deeds], *doing wonders* [miracles]?" (Exod. 15:11, KJV). Two other related nouns are mahalal and hillulim. Mahalal occurs once (prov. 27:21) and denotes the degree of "praise" or its lack. Hillulim, which occurs twice, means "festal jubilation" in the fourth year at harvest time (Lev. 19:24, RSV; Judg. 9:27, NASB).

c) Word: **todah**

    i) Strong's Number: 8426

    ii) Part of Speech: Noun

    iii) Usage Notes: "thanksgiving." This important noun form, found some 30 times in the Old Testament, is used there in the sense of "thanksgiving." The word is preserved in modern Hebrew as the regular word for "thanks." In the Hebrew text todah is used to indicate "thanksgiving" in songs of worship (Psa. 26:7; Psa. 42:4). Sometimes the word is used to refer to the thanksgiving choir or procession (Neh. 12:31, 38). One of the peace offerings, or "sacrings," was designated the thanksgiving offering (Lev. 7:12

The sound of this Hebrew word spoken in North American slang represents the fanfare of a circus orchestra which is played after each performer has accomplished something worthy of applause. It is most interesting to me how this word can mean "thanksgiving choir or processional," which, to me, causes images to form in my mind of this choir and processional doing the same thing for God that the circus orchestra does for the performers, announcing that God has done something worthy of our thanks and praise.

Chapter Five

Intimate, Passionate Worship

God Desires an Intimate Relationship with Mankind

Mankind was created to have a relationship with our Creator. Without a relationship with God, our existence is incomplete. We were not created to exist apart from God. God holds our very lives in the palm of His hand.

> "Who among all these does not know that the hand of the Lord has done this, in Whose hand is the life of every living **thing**, and the breath of all **mankind**?" (Job 12:9–10, NKJV).

This is the conclusion of one of Job's speeches to his friends. Job explained how everything on the earth was created by almighty God. This conclusion boldly declares that every living creature knows they were created and given life and purpose by their Creator, God. Not only is all of life created by God; all of life on this earth is also maintained by God, who holds all our lives in His very hands.

You should remember this Scripture we discussed in the first chapter of this book. Let's read it again to remind us of what it says and our study of it. However, this time, let us read the very next short verse as well. You will see immediately how God's responsibility to His creation does not stop with the mere creation of life. As Job concluded, God is also the one who maintains all of life.

"For by him were all things created, that are in heaven, and that are in earth, visible and invisible, whether they be thrones, or dominions, or principalities, or powers: all things were created by him, and for him: And he is before all things, and **by him all things consist.***" (Colossians 1:16–17, KJV).*

This means that all of creation is in a dependent relationship with its creator—whether it knows or likes this fact or not. God holds our very lives in His hands. He gave us life so He could have a progressive relationship with all His creation. God's heart for His relationship with us is that it would progress way beyond a "Creator/created" relationship. God wants this relationship with Himself and us to become very close. Here is the level of intimacy God declared through Jeremiah that He desires with us:

"For as the girdle cleaveth to the loins of a man, so have I caused to cleave unto Me the whole house of Israel and the whole house of Judah, saith the LORD; that they might be unto Me for a people, and for a name, and for a **praise,** *and for a* **glory***: but they would not hear." (Jeremiah 13:11, NKJV).*

Here's the way this Scripture reads in *The Revised Standard Version* of the Bible:

"For as the loincloth clings to one's loins, so I made the whole house of Israel and the whole house of Judah cling to Me, says the LORD, in order that they might be for Me a people, a name, a praise, and a glory. But they would not listen." (Jeremiah 13:11, RSV).

In *The Living Bible*, it reads:

"Even as a loincloth clings to a man's loins, so I made Judah and Israel to cling to Me, says the Lord." (Jeremiah 13:11, Living)

No matter how you look at it, God is describing an incredibly intimate relationship that He desires to have with us. As a matter of fact, I don't think you could describe a more intimate relationship than this.

God wants you and me to be as close to Him as underwear is to us.

I'll just let you think about that one for a while. There doesn't seem to be any more I can say about it right now, except to reiterate that God really wants a close relationship with us! It is this type of relationship which positions us to be considered God's people, who are called by His name to show forth the praise of His glory throughout all the earth.

It takes some time to develop that close of relationship with God, but that's the goal. To the degree our intimate relationship has developed with Jesus is the level we are able to express our love to Him.

Biblical Relationships between God and Man

God gives us natural relationships so we can learn how we are to relate to Him as we grow. Yet, none of these natural relationships should ever take the place of our growing, loving relationship with our Creator.

Also, our relationship with God is never to be a peer relationship. God and humanity are not equal. The Bible describes mankind's relationship with God in several ways. Here are a few of these directly quoted or implied biblical ways to describe God's desired relationship with mankind.

Biblical Relationships with God

God	us
Creator	Creation
Deity	Humanity
Savior	Sinner
Teacher	Student
King	Subject
Lord	Servant
Master	Bond-slave
Strong one	Weak one
Independent	Dependent
Friend	Friend
Father	Son/child

Table 8

Jesus Creates Every Person Out of Love

Of all these relationships, my favorite type is that of being a child of my heavenly Father. A son or daughter is created by his or her father, mother, and God. If the parents love each other, the child—who is the offspring of that parental love relationship—will also be loved by the parents. However, even if we were born to natural parents who did not love each other, let alone their offspring, our heavenly Father—who created us in our natural mother's womb—made us out of love. It is impossible for God to not love. Our Creator is the epitome of love—He *is* love!

> "Behold, what manner of love the Father hath bestowed upon us, that we should be called the sons of God: therefore the world knoweth us not, because it knew Him not." (1 John 3:1, KJV).

> "Beloved, let us love one another: for love is of God; and every one that loveth is born of God, and knoweth God. He that loveth not knoweth not God; for God is love." (1 John 4:7–8, KJV).

Even if our natural parents did not conceive us from a loving relationship, it is impossible for life to exist without God forming it in the womb. Therefore, every one of us was created from love.

> "Then the word of the LORD came unto me, saying, Before I formed thee in the belly I knew thee; and before thou camest forth out of the womb I sanctified thee, and I ordained thee a prophet unto the nations." (Jeremiah 1:4–5, KJV).

> "And now the LORD says—He who formed me in the womb to be His servant, to bring Jacob back to Him, and gather Israel to Himself, for I am honored in the eyes of the LORD, and my God has been my strength—He says: "It is too small a thing for you to be my servant." (Isaiah 49:5–6, NIV).

Although we are created and called to be servants of the Most High, servanthood doesn't totally describe the relationship God wants with us. God wants a loving relationship with us. He wants children who will receive His love and then express love back to Him of their own free will.

The Father/Child Relationship

The best relationship of all those we have listed above in which this love relationship could be accomplished is a parent/child relationship. In that relationship, we see aspects of almost all of the other relationships listed. We have already spoken of how parents create life in conjunction with God. God is called our Father. A good father is a child's most important and influential teacher. A father is king of his castle, lord of his home, and master or steward of his world. He's the strong one on whom his children can depend. A father is also a friend to his children. It is in the progressive parent/child relationship that love can flourish—love being expressed from God to His children and from God's children back to God.

The expression of love from mankind to God is called worship. Worship is reserved as expressions of love to God only. Worship is never to be used to express love to other people, objects, or beings, such as angels.

Relationships Are to Progress and Develop

A relationship between you and God is to be a progressive one, just like all natural relationships will also develop. Our relationship with the Lord may start with us being His servants or slaves, but God is going to continue to move our relationships with Him deeper, based on love, not just a commitment. God wants sons and daughters. If all He wanted was servants, He would have stopped after He created the angels. After all, you can be a friend with your child, but seldom does it work to be friends with your servant.

> "Henceforth I call you not servants; for the servant knoweth not what his lord doeth: but I have called you friends; for all things that I have heard of My Father I have made known unto you." (John 15:15, KJV).

A friend confides in a friend. We see how God desires man's relationship with Him to be based on love and trust and expects this loving relationship to be progressive, with both ever growing closer together.

Progression into a Marriage Relationship with God

There is one more type of relationship mentioned in the Bible that God desires with mankind which I didn't include in the list above. It is the ultimate loving relationship—that of a bride and a groom.

> *"For this cause shall a man leave his father and mother, and shall be joined unto his wife, and they two shall be one flesh. This is a great mystery: but I speak concerning Christ and the church." (Ephesians 5:31–32, KJV).*

Although God longs for the parent/child relationship with mankind above the other relationships we have listed, He ultimately desires for us to grow in our understanding of Him in such a way that we can begin to relate to Him as our lover and marriage partner. We see, then, that our relationship with God is intended to grow or progress from "Lord/servant" to "husband/wife" within our lifetime here on earth.

A natural marriage relationship should be much more than a relationship of service to the object of our love, although serving our spouse must always be a part of a husband-and-wife relationship if it is to succeed. Likewise, our relationship with our Creator must start with us confessing that Jesus is our Lord; but it should progress to a marriage relationship.

> *"That if you confess with your mouth, "Jesus is Lord," and believe in your heart that God raised Him from the dead, you will be saved." (Romans 10:9, NKJV).*

Salvation is the starting place of a relationship between mankind and God. A salvation relationship happens when we realize we are sinners, and we need a Savior who will save us from our sins. To accept Jesus as our Savior, we must declare a commitment to Him as our Lord. By the way, if Jesus is Lord, then that makes us His servants. Therefore, according to Romans 10:9, we add to our Savior/sinner relationship with God the Lord/servant relationship. This does not mean that Jesus ceases to be our Savior when He becomes our Lord. He is both to us—so it is with every developmental stage of our relationship with our God. Each relationship aspect is added to the previous ones, and they are never abandoned.

A marriage relationship must go beyond friendship; however, it is vital to a marriage that a couple be best of friends. So it should be with our Lord as well. We need to develop a friendship relationship with Jesus and add it to our servant relationship with Him. "

> "A man that hath friends must shew himself friendly: and there is a Friend that sticketh closer than a brother." (Proverbs 18:24, KJV).

A marriage relationship must go way beyond a covenant commitment of a husband and wife to each other; yet, without this commitment, a marriage does not exist. When we declare that Jesus is Lord, it is our covenant commitment to our God that we will pursue a progressive relationship with Him for the rest of our lives.

A married couple expresses their love to each other on intimate levels—mentally, emotionally, and physically. This marriage intimacy can also reach into the spiritual realm if the marriage partners are both in relationship with their Creator.

Remember the people Paul wrote about in Romans 1 who got on that downward spiral away from God. They knew God at one time, but I suspect they probably only knew Him as their master or Lord. They were probably only God's servants, not His friends, children, or marriage partners. It is a safe assumption that they never experienced the expressing of love to God in an intimate way. They probably were just expressing their love to God out of duty, not from a growing, loving relationship with God.

The Marriage Act and the Worship Act

God has ordained the marriage bed for many reasons.

"Marriage is honourable in all, and the bed undefiled: but whoremongers and adulterers God will judge." (Hebrews 13:4, KJV).

The most obvious reason God has given us the marriage bed is procreation of the human race. However, sex God's way is also an important part of realizing and maintaining a trusting, open relationship between husband and wife. When the marriage bed is established by a loving relationship between man and wife, it becomes impossible for that couple to experience the marriage act continually and maintain deception between each other. This is why God is so adamant about us staying sexually pure until marriage. He wants that safeguard built into our marriage.

Casual sex totally undermines this safeguard which God intended for us. It also insures that we will never experience sex the way God desires for us—short of a miracle. The marriage act is meant to be a union between a man and wife on all levels of our beings—physical, mental, emotional, and spiritual. Casual sex, short of a miracle, insures that we will only experience this marriage act on the physical level—and only into the mental level in a perverted way. Of course, the marriage act will always touch everyone's emotions in one way or another; however, we cannot experience the marriage act in a healthy emotional way, short of a miracle, once we have given ourselves to casual sex. In other words, by not approaching our sexuality the way God intended for us, we can severely lose the perspective which God intended for us to have concerning our sex lives.

At the risk of being too graphic with my words, it is important that we understand that God intends for us to progress to the place in our worship relationship with Him in which we expend as much physical energy while we worship Him as would be expended in the marriage bed. After all, God has ordained this type of physical intimacy between a man and wife, and this relationship is His picture to us of how He wants to be loved by us in our act of worship.

"The wild animals honor Me, the jackals and the owls, because I provide water in the desert, and streams in the wasteland, to give drink to My people, My chosen, the people

I formed for Myself that they may proclaim My praise. Yet you have not called upon Me, O Jacob, you have not wearied yourselves for Me, O Israel." (Isaiah 43:20–22, NIV).

We are told here that God wants us to express our love to Him with every ounce of energy we have, not holding back anything. God wants us to weary ourselves in our act of worship, just as we would weary ourselves from passion in the expression of our love to our spouse.

"And one of the scribes came, and having heard them reasoning together, and perceiving that He had answered them well, asked Him, Which is the first commandment of all? And Jesus answered him, The first of all the commandments is, Hear, O Israel; The Lord our God is one Lord: and thou shalt love the Lord thy God with all thy heart, and with all thy soul, and with all thy mind, and with all thy strength: this is the first commandment." (Mark 12:28–30, KJV).

If you are using all of your strength when expressing your love to God, you will be weary when you are through. I guess a good test to know if you have worshiped God the way He wants to be worshiped is to see how weary you are at the end of your worship time. Of course, the older I get, the less strength I seem to have in the natural. Strength is relative to each individual.

Passionate Worshipers Are Passionately Obedient

We have seen that our worship of God needs to have two important qualities: intimacy and passion. Without these two qualities, our worship is not biblical worship. Plus, it is difficult to continuously weary ourselves in the expression of our love to God unless we are motivated by hearts full of passionate love for our Lord. It is the passion that creates the intimacy which we and God long for. Without passion for the presence of God, our acts of worship toward God become dead, empty works.

Intimacy and passion are the results of an obedient relationship with almighty God—the servant/Lord relationship. In other words, our relationship with God grows and develops into intimacy and passion, but at first, we will simply express our love for Him as an act of obedience to what He has commanded of us. However, intimacy is achieved more quickly when we adopt a wholehearted attitude to our obedience.

> *"Servants, obey in all things your masters according to the flesh; not with eyeservice, as menpleasers; but in singleness of heart, fearing God: and whatsoever ye do, do it heartily, as to the Lord, and not unto men." (Colossians 3:22–23, KJV).*

We should do what God wants or has commanded to the glory of God with everything we've got—our whole bodies, or strength; our complete souls, which includes our emotions and our minds; and our spirits, or our whole hearts. This is the indisputable evidence of passion—doing something heartily. It is when we weary ourselves in the act of obeying God that we demonstrate our passionate love for Him.

The Results of Non-Passionate Obedience

This is a sad story, but one we must read if we want to understand the potential devastation which will enter our lives if we live without Godly passion.

> *"Elisha had become sick with the illness of which he would die. Then Joash the king of Israel came down to him, and wept over his face, and said, "O my father, my father, the chariots of Israel and their horsemen!" And Elisha said to him, "Take a bow and some arrows." So he took himself a bow and some arrows. Then he said to the king of Israel, "Put your hand on the bow." So he put his hand on it, and Elisha put his hands on the king's hands. And he said, "Open the east window"; and he opened it. Then Elisha said, "Shoot"; and he shot. And he said, "The arrow of the Lord's deliverance and the arrow of deliverance from Syria; for you must strike the Syrians at Aphek till you have destroyed them." Then he said, "Take the arrows"; so he took them. And he said to the king of Israel, "Strike the ground"; so he struck three times, and stopped. And the man of God was angry with him, and said, "You should have struck five or six*

times; then you would have struck Syria till you had destroyed it! But now you will strike Syria only three times." (2 Kings 13:14–19, NKJV).

The first thing about a non-passionate person we notice in this Scripture is how self-centered he or she is. The writer of 2 Kings tells us that the prophet Elisha was on his death bed and was very sick. There is something very noticeable about a person who is sick and dying. If you've ever been around when someone is "sick unto death," you know it is very difficult to ignore the sense of impending death. It takes a totally self-engrossed person to not notice that something is different. I believe God gives us this sensitivity at times near death to both warn those of us still living that the time is near and to prepare the person who is about to leave this world.

King Joash demonstrated absolutely zero sensitivity to the sick and dying Elisha. When I first read this story—the fact that Joash made a point of traveling to where Elisha was and that Joash went in and started weeping over Elisha's face—I was thinking that these were demonstrations of love and respect toward Elisha. I anticipated to read next that Joash begged God to not take the prophet away from Israel.

But instead, Joash wasn't concerned about Elisha at all. Joash only wanted to use him to hear from God about what he was facing. I submit that the actions of the king to weep over Elisha's face as Elisha was dying was the epitome of disrespect and insensitivity.

In this story, we see grace in Elisha to not get upset with Joash—as opposed to his early years in ministry, when he called bears to kill a bunch of kids who called him "bald-head." Elisha, motivated by his love for God and Israel, put aside any offense in order to hear from God on Israel's behalf. Also, although he was weak from his sickness, he still acted and spoke with great passion.

The first prophetic act God told Elisha to have Joash do was to shoot an arrow out of the window. As the arrow went flying, God revealed His heart toward Israel, and declared, *"The arrow of the Lord's deliverance and the arrow of deliverance from Syria; for you must strike the Syrians at Aphek till you have destroyed them."*

That is an awesome promise from God. Who would not want to receive such a prophetic word? God just told Joash, by using a dying man, that Israel would defeat its enemy by *destroying* it. This is an awesome promise! With that kind of insurance of victory, Israel could march boldly into war, knowing they would not just win a battle or two, but the war.

God had a test for king Joash to see how empowered he had allowed himself to become by that promise. Elisha instructed Joash to pick up the rest of his arrows and strike the ground with them. A passionate person does not know excess. There is no such thing as "too much" for a person of passion. Passionate obedience to this Word of the Lord would probably look something like one or more of these:

1. striking the ground so hard and so many times that the arrows begin to break
2. holding the arrows so tight from hitting them so hard and so many times on the ground that your knuckles turn white, and when you finally quit from sheer exhaustion, someone has to pry your fingers from around the arrows
3. striking your knuckles along with the arrows so hard on the ground and so many times that they start to bleed, yet not stopping
4. the thunderous, repetitive sounds of striking the ground draws people from blocks around to find out what is happening
5. continuing to strike the ground until you have to change hands several times in order to keep going
6. panting for breath from the extreme physical exertion, yet having no thought of giving up

It is interesting to me that, although this is what passion looks like, God would have accepted five or six good strikes on the ground as proof of passion. In other words, we should be prepared to weary ourselves, but understand that God is not as impressed with the strikes we make on the ground as He is with our willingness to obey Him passionately from our hearts.

So what was the result of non-passionate obedience to God's commandment?

> "And the man of God was angry with him, and said, 'You should have struck five or six times; then you would have

*struck Syria till you had destroyed it! But now you will strike
Syria only three times.'" (2 Kings 13:19, NKJV).*

Incredible as this may seem, Joash's lack of passion totally negated the
original promise from God to him. Our lack of passion will keep us from
realizing God's best for us. Everything we do—especially our obedience
to God's will and Word—must be done with the whole heart, soul, and
might. Otherwise, God will have nothing to do with us. Moderation in
our obedience of God's will has this effect on Him:

> *"And to the angel of the church of the Laodiceans write,
> 'These things says the Amen, the Faithful and True Witness,
> the Beginning of the creation of God: I know your works,
> that you are neither cold nor hot. I could wish you were cold
> or hot. So then, because you are lukewarm, and neither cold
> nor hot, I will vomit you out of My mouth." (Revelation
> 3:14–16, NKJV).*

Keep in mind that the Lord is addressing the works, or actions of
the church of the Laodiceans. He said to them that their actions are not
extreme—cold or hot—but their works are only moderate, or lukewarm.
Since there is no extreme passion being expressed by their actions, God
is repulsed by them. Just like a drink of water is great either cold or hot,
lukewarm water is spit out, because it does not satisfy. When our actions
demonstrate half-heartedness, they are repulsive to God. God wants us
to be people of passion! When we worship Him, we do it with every part
of our beings—*never* in moderation!

A Word of Balance

If you are in a church or denomination that does not have this
revelation about expressing our love passionately with all our beings—
especially our strength—*do not* offend them by expressing your love to
God with exuberance within that corporate setting of worship. Let your
private times of worship reflect this principle of passion, but only express
your worship to God in your church's corporate worship settings at the
level which will not offend your fellow worshipers.

"So whatever you believe about these things keep between yourself and God. Blessed is the man who does not condemn himself by what he approves." (Romans 14:22, NIV).

Having passion is not an option in your private worship times. It, however, is not your right to worship with extreme passion in a corporate worship gathering where the leadership is uncomfortable with it. Please walk in wisdom concerning this, being patient with your church to grasp this biblical concept.

Chapter Six

The Presence of God

Psalm 100—An Exposé of Biblical Worship

In my opinion, this short, five-verse chapter encapsulates several biblical basics of worship. Take the time to read the entire chapter.

> *"Make a joyful shout to the Lord, all you lands! Serve the Lord with gladness; come before His presence with singing. Know that the Lord, He is God; it is He who has made us, and, not we ourselves; we are His people and the sheep of His pasture. Enter into His gates with thanksgiving, and into His courts with praise. Be thankful to Him, and bless His name. For the Lord is good; His mercy is everlasting, and His truth endures to all generations."* (Psalm 100:1–5, NKJV).

It is not my purpose to exegete this entire chapter, but I do want to point out two things. First, the presence of God is identified in Psalm 100:2 as the goal of biblical worship—to come before His presence with worship. Worship is not our goal; worship is the means to realize our goal, which is to enter the presence of God.

With that established, we can examine Psalm 100:4, which outlines for us the first two steps we take to accomplish the goal of entering God's presence. These steps are first likened to approaching God's dwelling place. First, we go through His gates; then we enter His courtyard. Going through the gates is done by giving God thanks. Entering His courtyard is done by giving God praise.

Then, for greater clarity of what is being said, the Psalmist repeated this all again in a different way in the last phrase of Psalm 100:4: *"Be thankful to Him, and bless His name."*

To bless God is to praise Him. But biblical worship begins with a thankful heart attitude. We must be thankful—as the rhyme goes, have "an attitude of gratitude." The expression of praise to God starts with a thankful heart.

According to Psalm 100:4, the first two steps we take to come before God's presence are explained to us in three different ways.

Come Before His Presence

Step 1	Step 2
Enter His gates	Enter His courts
with thanksgiving	with praise
Be thankful	Bless His name

Table 9

Remember, having hearts full of thanks is the first step we take toward the presence of God.

Worship Springs from a Thankful Attitude

Romans 1 describes for us the downward regression of degradation which will occur in people who choose to not glorify God.

> *"Because that, when they knew God, they glorified Him not as God, neither were thankful; but became vain in their imaginations, and their foolish heart was darkened." (Romans 1:21, KJV).*

Even if we know God, if we choose not to worship God, we will become unthankful. When that happens, we are one step away from the downward regression which Paul outlines for us in Romans 1. Here is a diagram which overlays Romans 1 with Psalm 100:4 and demonstrates that all Christian growth begins with a thankful attitude.

Psalms 100:2,4 / Romans 1:21

Know God/
God's Presence

Praise/
Glorify God   3   3 Glorified Him
                              NOT as God
        Be   2   2 Neither were
    Thankful   1 Thankful
            1   Vain
                          Imaginations
Steps   Heart
to   Steps -1
Growth   to   Darkened
               Backsliding -2 v.24 Dishonor
                          Their Bodies
                        -3   v.26 Vile
                            Affections
                         -4 v.28 Reprobate
                              Mind
                              -5

Paul identifies the people he is referring to in Romans chapter one as people who at one time "knew God." What started their backsliding away from God was their choice to stop worshiping God. The result of this decision to stop worshiping God was an <u>unthankful</u> attitude, which then validated to the person his or her choice to stop worshiping God. To reverse this unthankfulness requires a choice once again to worship God.

If we determine to have thankful attitudes toward God, the next step in our positive spiritual growth is to choose to be a worshiper to glorify God. As we worship the Lord as a "sacrifice of praise," our attitudes will eventually change, and we will become thankful.

We will discuss this next point later in this chapter, but let me simply introduce this topic now. The result of choosing to be a worshiper goes both directions on the stairs. Not only will we become thankful, but we also will begin to know God more. In other words, biblical worship will always result in God revealing Himself to us a little more than He has before.

In Romans 1, however, these people did not cultivate thankful attitudes by choosing to glorify the Lord as God; instead, they gave place to backsliding, which touched all three parts of their beings—spirit, soul, and body—as well as all three parts of their souls—mind, will, and emotions. Study this chart below to understand this more fully.

Backsliding will Touch Every Part of us!

Romans 1 Effects of Backsliding	Part of Human Being Affected
v.21 became vain in their imaginations	by acts of their **will**—part of the soul
v.21 their foolish heart was darkened	a person's heart is the **spirit**
v. 24 to dishonor their own bodies	obviously the human **body**
v. 26 unto vile affections	affections are **emotions**—part of the soul
v. 28 to a reprobate mind	obviously the **mind**—part of the soul

Table 10

This backward sliding away from knowing God also reveals how Adam and Eve's sin permeated all parts of man's being, making it necessary for God to implement a redemption plan that would redeem all three parts of mankind—spirit, soul, and body.

We said in chapter five of this book that our relationship with God needs to be a progressive one, always growing into new levels of knowing God. No one stays in the same place for very long on the staircase of life. To live is to grow in one direction or the other. The direction our lives will take will be determined when we answer the question, "Will we be a worshiper of God?" Our answer to this question sets us in motion—either up toward knowing the presence of God or down toward a reprobate mind. To choose to not worship God will result in an unthankful attitude, which will open us up to a slippery slope to hell.

God's Goal for Us Is that We Would Know Him

We have outlined the biblical results which happen when we choose to glorify and worship God. The result of true biblical worship is to enter God's presence, where we will know God in a greater way. In other words, worship is the means to an end. Worship is not the goal of our lives; knowing God and His presence is the goal. Worship is the vitally important way to reach that goal.

The result of a lifelong pursuit to be a worshiper of our Lord Jesus Christ is to know God. Every time we worship God, He reveals Himself to us a little bit more—so much so that spiritual maturity is equated with knowing God.

> "I write unto you, little children, because your sins are forgiven you for His name's sake. I write unto you, fathers, because ye have known Him that is from the beginning. I write unto you, young men, because ye have overcome the wicked one." (1 John 2:12–13, KJV).

The most important revelation to a child in the faith is that his or her sins are forgiven through the cross and resurrection of Jesus, our Lord. This act by the Lord reveals just how much God loves us.

> "But God commendeth His love toward us, in that, while we were yet sinners, Christ died for us." (Romans 5:8, KJV).

Therefore, the greatest revelation for a babe in Christ is that Jesus loves him or her so much that He died for them so their sins can be forgiven. Can you remember when the love of Christ was the most important revelation about God in your life? I hope you can. I hope you never forget that!

Also, you can always spot an adolescent in the faith when he or she is moving into the revelation from God about his or her authority in Christ over sin, the devil, and his demons. Of course, just like natural teenagers, spiritual young people can also think that they know everything there is to know when they have received the revelation of these truths. Some can even get very aggressive about this revelation in an effort to exhort those younger in Christ to continue to grow. Spiritual adolescents can almost seem condemning of those who have not received these revelations yet. However, that is not the major concern for these teenagers in the Spirit. The most dangerous temptation at this level of growth is to stay focused on overcoming the evil one because of the quick results and personal satisfaction realized through spiritual warfare. It is desired for us that we all progress, adding to this important revelation the knowledge of who God is.

A true father or mother in the faith can be recognized by his or her passion to simply know God more than anything else!

Here is a review of the biblical outline of the pursuit of spiritual maturity found in 1 John 2.

John's Outline of Christian Growth

Who	Biblical phrase	their revelation
little children	*your sins are forgiven*	God's love
young men	*ye have overcome the wicked one*	spiritual warfare
fathers	*ye have known him that is from the beginning*	knowing God

Table 11

How to Know God

How do we get to know God? Quite simply, the more time you spend with someone, the more you will know them. So it is with God. The more time you spend in His presence, the more you will know Him.

Yes, it is true that you can get to know a lot *about* somebody by reading what he or she has written, just as we can learn much about God from the Bible. However, ask any husband or wife with a spouse in the military who has been separated for a period of time by a dangerous tour of duty if the letters, e-mails, or phone calls from his or her spouse during that time made up for the personal contact with the other person. There is no substitute for being with someone when it comes to getting to know them. So it is with God; we must spend time in His presence to get to know Him.

How do we get into the presence of God? We do it by functioning as we were created to function—we praise and worship the Lord. The Bible makes it clear that God reveals His presence when we praise Him.

"But Thou art holy, O Thou that inhabitest the praises of Israel." (Psalm 22:3, KJV).

God's presence inhabits, or abides in, the praises of Israel. By the way, *true Israel* is not the nationality of Jews found around the world. The true Israeli nation is made up of all the true worshipers in the world. The true mark of an Israelite is not the physical circumcision the Jews are known for; circumcision is to be of the heart.

"For we are the circumcision, which worship God in the spirit, and rejoice in Christ Jesus, and have no confidence in the flesh." (Philippians 3:3, KJV).

"For he is not a Jew, which is one outwardly; neither is that circumcision, which is outward in the flesh: But he is a Jew, which is one inwardly; and circumcision is that of the heart, in the spirit, and not in the letter; whose praise is not of men, but of God." (Romans 2:28–29, KJV).

We see that the most mature Christians will be worshipers—those who spend time in God's presence getting to know Him.

Practicing the Presence of God

I remember when I yielded to God's will to attend university and study music. Before I attended any classes, I thought I knew quite a bit about music—at least, enough to function in music ministry. However, the more I learned about music, the more I realized I did not know about music. Finally, when it was time to graduate from university, I did not want to leave school. After six intensive years of training, I felt like I knew relatively nothing about music. However, my appetite for music knowledge had become acute to the degree that I felt the years of music training at the university level were just a drop in the bucket of musical knowledge available, and I wanted more!

The identifiable mark of a maturing Christian is his or her hunger to know God in a more intimate way than he or she knows Him now. We can see this insatiable hunger to know God in Paul's letter to the Philippians, written after he had walked with God for most of his life.

> "That I may **know** Him, and the power of His resurrection, and the fellowship of His sufferings, being made conformable unto His death." (Philippians 3:10, KJV).

How can a man like Paul come down to the last years of his life, after walking with God closer than most of us have, and still cry out to know God more? I believe it is because there is so much of God to know, it is impossible for anyone to completely know God in his or her lifetime on earth. I believe we will continue to receive revelation of God, even after we join the worship of God going on in heaven after we pass from this world.

Jesus indicated to His disciples as He was leaving earth that He had only begun to reveal to them all He wanted to show them of Himself. He assured them that, even after He left them on earth, He would keep on revealing Himself to them by the presence of His Holy Spirit.

> "I have yet many things to say unto you, but ye cannot bear them now. Howbeit when he, the Spirit of truth, is come, he will guide you into all truth: for he shall not speak of himself; but whatsoever he shall hear, that shall he speak: and he will shew you things to come. He shall glorify me: for he shall receive of mine, and shall shew it unto you. All things that the Father hath are mine: therefore said I, that he shall take of mine, and shall shew it unto you." (John 16:12-15, KJV)

Why does God not reveal everything about Himself that He wants us to know in one moment of time? There are two reasons for this. First, we cannot bear them all at one time. Only God knows how much of Himself each of us can bear at any given time. As we continue to spend time in His presence, we become capable of handling more and more of His presence—just like when we physically exercise and increase our capacity for more exercise. If I tried to run a marathon right now, I would kill myself. My body is not conditioned to handle that much exercise at this time. Likewise, no person can handle a complete revelation of God at one time. That much of God would kill us. Notice in this conversation between Moses and the Lord how this is brought out.

> "If Thy **presence** go not with me, carry us not up hence.
>
> For wherein shall it be known here that I and Thy people have found grace in Thy sight? is it not in that Thou goest with us? so shall we be separated, I and Thy people, from all the people that are upon the face of the earth.
>
> And the LORD said unto Moses, "I will do this thing also that thou hast spoken: for thou hast found grace in My sight, and I know thee by name."
>
> And he said, "I beseech thee, shew me Thy **glory**."
>
> And He said, "I will make all My goodness pass before thee, and I will proclaim the name of the LORD before thee; and will be gracious to whom I will be gracious, and will shew mercy on whom I will shew mercy."
>
> And He said, "thou canst not see My face: for there shall no man see Me, and live. And the LORD said, "Behold, there is a place by Me, and thou shalt stand upon a rock, And it shall come to pass, while My glory passeth by, that I will put thee in a clift of the rock, and will cover thee with My hand while I pass by: And I will take away Mine hand, and thou shalt see My back parts: but My face shall not be seen." (Exodus 33:13–23, KJV).

God knew just how much of Himself Moses could handle at that time, and that's how much of His glory God revealed to Moses. However, Moses had spent enough time in the presence of God that his being was conditioned to handle more of God than Aaron and all the children of Israel could handle. When the Israelites witnessed how the presence of God physically affected Moses, they were afraid.

> *"And it came to pass, when Moses came down from Mount Sinai with the two tables of testimony in Moses' hand, when he came down from the mount, that Moses wist not that the skin of his face shone while he talked with Him. And when Aaron and all the children of Israel saw Moses, behold, the skin of his face shone; and they were afraid to come nigh him."* (Exodus 34:29–30, KJV).

Therefore, God wants us to condition ourselves every day to increase our capacity to contain His presence and further revelation of Himself. How do we increase our physical strength? We exercise. How do we increase our capacity for the presence of God? We spend time worshiping Him, for His presence abides in our worship of Him. We practice God's presence by worshiping Him.

The Desire for God

The second reason God does not reveal Himself completely to us at one time is because He wants us to desire Him. It is difficult and wrong to share yourself with another person if he or she does not have the desire to know you. As we grow in our relationships here on earth, we find ourselves opening up to the one or two people who show interest in who we are. We don't walk up to a total stranger and begin telling that person our life story—at least, most of us don't, and all of us shouldn't.

All relationships develop over a period of time. We share more of ourselves with others when they indicate genuine, wholehearted, continual interest in us. This is also how it is in a relationship with God. God has chosen to reveal himself to those who seek Him with their whole hearts on a continual basis. In fact, He has promised to be found by us when we meet these conditions as we seek Him.

> *"But you will also begin to search again for Jehovah your God, and you will find Him when you search for Him with all your heart and soul."* (Deuteronomy 4:29, TLB).

Why did God only mention seeking Him with our hearts and souls and not our bodies? In this life on earth, our bodies are waiting for the day of adoption, when they will be changed to be like the Lord's glorious body. In our beings, if the Spirit is in control, we will seek God, and our bodies will follow its lead. However, if the Spirit does not give leadership, the body will resume that position of leadership and draw us away from God to the desires of the flesh. In other words, it is impossible for our bodies to seek after God while on this earth. We must simply crucify our flesh, bring our bodies under subjection, make them living sacrifices, and not cater to the desires of our bodies.

> "I love them that love Me; and those that seek Me early shall find Me." (Proverbs 8:17, KJV).

As independent people, our tendency is to only seek God after we have tried to meet a challenge with our own might. By then, we are usually in need of an extremely major miracle. This is considered as seeking God late into the need. What God wants is that we would seek Him early—even first—and that all of our seeking Him would be from the standpoint of wanting to know Him in that particular situation.

> "And ye shall seek Me, and find Me, when ye shall search for Me with all your heart." (Jeremiah 29:13, KJV).

God does not want to hide Himself from us. He wants to reveal Himself to us. In fact, God wants to reveal Himself more than we want Him to reveal Himself. Therefore, He has required that we do not seek Him halfheartedly. He has promised to be found by us when we seek Him.

> "Ask, and it shall be given you; seek, and ye shall find; knock, and it shall be opened unto you: For every one that asketh receiveth; and he that seeketh findeth; and to him that knocketh it shall be opened." (Matthew 7:7–8, KJV).

How badly do we want to know God? To the degree that we seek God with our hearts and souls, God will reveal Himself to us. Yet, when we seek God with total desperation to know Him, we are placing in His hands the decision as to how much of Himself or His presence He feels we can handle at that moment.

Isaiah's Revelation of God

People who are full of themselves very seldom seek God with their whole hearts and souls. Because of this, sometimes God will simply reveal Himself to them out of mercy, to give them a taste of His presence. He does this so they will hunger for more of His presence and begin seeking Him out of desperation. This is what happened in Isaiah's life.

Isaiah was a young preacher in the adolescent stage of his relationship with God when God, by His mercy, revealed Himself to Isaiah. Notice the accusatory attitude in Isaiah 5. Notice how Isaiah declares woe upon those engaged in sins which he felt should have no hold on those committing these sins. This is typical of a teenager in the faith who has received the revelation of how to overcome the wicked one.

> "**Woe** unto them that join house to house, that lay field to field, till there be no place, that they may be placed alone in the midst of the earth!

> **Woe** unto them that rise up early in the morning, that they may follow strong drink; that continue until night, till wine inflame them! And the harp, and the viol, the tabret, and pipe, and wine, are in their feasts: but they regard not the work of the LORD, neither consider the operation of His hands.

> **Woe** unto them that draw iniquity with cords of vanity, and sin as it were with a cart rope: That say, Let him make speed, and hasten his work, that we may see it: and let the counsel of the Holy One of Israel draw nigh and come, that we may know it! **Woe** unto them that call evil good, and good evil; that put darkness for light, and light for darkness; that put bitter for sweet, and sweet for bitter! **Woe** unto them that are wise in their own eyes, and prudent in their own sight! **Woe** unto them that are mighty to drink wine, and men of strength to mingle strong drink: Which justify the wicked for reward, and take away the righteousness of the righteous from Him!

Therefore is the anger of the LORD kindled against His people, and He hath stretched forth His hand against them, and hath smitten them: and the hills did tremble, and their carcasses were torn in the midst of the streets. For all this His anger is not turned away, but His hand is stretched out still." (Isaiah 5:8, 11–12, 18–22, 25, KJV).

God, in His mercy, did not leave Isaiah in that state. In the very next chapter, we see Isaiah become a completely different person, because God revealed Himself to Isaiah.

"In the year that king Uzziah died I saw also the Lord ① sitting upon a throne, high and lifted up, and His train② filled the temple. Above it stood the seraphims: each one had six wings; with twain he covered his face, and with twain he covered his feet, and with twain he did fly. And one cried unto another, and said, Holy, holy, holy, is the LORD of hosts: the whole earth③ is full of His glory. And the posts of the door moved at the voice of him that cried, and the house was filled with smoke.

Then said I, **Woe④** *is me! for I am undone; because I am a man of unclean lips, and I dwell in the midst of a people of unclean lips: for mine eyes have seen⑤ the King, the LORD of hosts.*

Then flew one of the seraphims unto me, having a live coal in his hand, which he had taken with the tongs from off the altar: and he laid it upon my mouth, ⑥ and said, Lo, this hath touched thy lips; and thine iniquity is taken away, and thy sin purged. Also I heard the voice of the Lord, saying, Whom shall I send, and who will go for Us? Then said I, here am I; ⑦ send me." (Isaiah 5:8, 11–12, 18–22, 25, KJV).

① For the worshiper, significant life changes toward the positive start with a revelation of God in some way. Isaiah's revelation came to him as a lifelike vision, some would say. However, I believe that God actually took Isaiah into heaven for this demonstration, since what Isaiah saw matches exactly what John and Paul saw when they visited heaven.

② The train of the Lord is the trail of His glory which follows Him. Solomon described it as smoke, while Moses saw it as a cloud by day and fire by night.

③ The revelation of God came to Isaiah in the context of worship, as it will also come to you and me. Notice the excitement in the angels over the earth being full of the glory of God, not heaven.

④ In Isaiah 5, Isaiah declared woe on everybody else. Once he had a true revelation of almighty God, he cried, "Woe is me!" In the context of worship, God will always reveal Himself to the worshiper who is seeking Him wholeheartedly. Once we receive a revelation of God, we will automatically receive a revelation of who we are in comparison to God. This revelation of ourselves will always convict us of our own sin and the sins that we've led others into, like those Isaiah confessed. At that point, we are no longer as concerned about other's sins as we are of our own sins as we cry out to God for mercy.

I believe that every time we purpose to worship God with our whole hearts, God will reveal a little more of Himself to us. I also believe that a true revelation of God will always cause us to see our own desperate state in comparison with God. I have found this to be the reason many Christians do not like to experience true worship. It causes them to see themselves in comparison to a holy God, and this is an uncomfortable place to be until we repent of our sins.

⑤ Again, why did Isaiah see himself as undone? Because his *"eyes [had] seen the King, the LORD of hosts."* The revelation of God makes it possible to have a true picture of ourselves in need of Him.

⑥ Once we confess our sins, not only are we forgiven, but God also sees to it that our desire to sin again does not exceed our desire to *not* have the "live coal experience" again. This two-step process which God has for dealing with sin in our lives is also outlined for us in 1 John 1:9 *"If we confess our sins, He is faithful and just to forgive us our sins, and to cleanse us from all unrighteousness."* (KJV).

If we confess, God will both forgive and cleanse. The cleansing process will be equivalent to having a live coal placed on our lips. It's the reason God instructed us to punish our children with imposed physical pain. The painful consequences of sin make us choose to not sin.

⑦ Once worship brings the revelation of God, followed by the revelation of ourselves—which produces a true repentance in us—then (and only then) are we ready to begin to minister to others.

The Isaiah pattern of worship found in this Scripture will also be discussed in more detail in the "Leading Worship" book.

The Worship Cycle

Every time we receive a greater revelation of God as we are worshiping Him, it inspires us to worship Him more. When we worship Him more, we receive a further revelation of God, which in turn inspires more worship from us to God. It becomes, then, a self-perpetuating cycle in which we become addicted to the very presence of God. Soon we cannot live without our daily encounter with God's presence.

Without the presence of God, we become desperate people—we have to know His presence to even survive on a daily basis! We will stop at nothing (within holiness) to have God's presence every day we live. Once again, God's presence is only experienced in the context of worship.

The Rain Cycle

This worship cycle is much like the natural rain cycle. Rain happens after moisture is evaporated from the earth by the sun, the moisture collects in clouds, and it is eventually released back to the earth as precipitation. In the worship cycle, worship rises from God's people to God. God then responds to that worship by revealing

The Worship Cycle

a little more of Himself to the worshiper(s). This then inspires greater worship from the worshiper(s), which in turn causes God to reveal Himself further.

Let's Review—Worship Is ...

Worship is the outward expression of our inward love for almighty God. True Christian worship is unique from all other world religions in that it springs from our love for God, which is based in a thankful attitude of the heart. In all other world religions, worship is motivated by a near-paralyzing fear of retaliation from the god(s) being worshiped.

The more we know who God in Jesus is, what He does, and why He does it, the more our worship will reflect our heart of love for God.

Ironically, the more we worship Jesus from this revelation of Himself, the more God will reveal Himself and His works to us. This deeper revelation of God will result in a fuller expression of worship to God, which starts this worship cycle over again in our lives.

Keep in mind that true worship is always preceded by the biblical process known as submitting to God, His Word, and the new revelation we have received of Him. As long as we live, this worship cycle should repeat itself in our lives until we see Jesus face-to-face.

Two Philosophies of Worship

It is important to briefly discuss the different results of this chapter's teachings on our corporate worship so we underline the importance of what we have shared in this chapter.

I see two basic worship philosophies in the body of Christ these days. One philosophy sees worship, as we have talked about in this chapter, as the means to the end of the presence of God. The other philosophy sees worship as a self-fulfilling goal and holds the quality of music and worship as more important than the experience of the presence of God in our worship time. To this philosophy, worship becomes the goal of our corporate gatherings, and the presence of God is simply the byproduct of our worship, not the goal of our worship.

Under both philosophies, we can experience an awesome visitation of the presence of the Lord and think that we both have the same philosophy regarding worship. The difference is that to one person, God's presence is the reason we worship; to the other person, God's presence is the bonus when we worship.

At first examination, there does not seem to be very much difference between these two philosophies—just a slightly different way of looking at the same thing. However, I have come to understand that our philosophical stance on this issue will make huge differences when it comes to the practical walking out of worship within our local churches.

When everything goes well in worship, here's how these two philosophies might judge that experience.

Two Philosophies of Worship—Table A

If worship is our goal, we might say:	If the presence of God is our goal, we might say:
"The worship was awesome today!"	"The presence of God was awesome today!"

Table 12

These statements are harmless and possibly could mean the same thing to two different people. However, the real test comes when the worship experience and presence of God are less than desirable. This is when these philosophies really stand out from each other. When we are troubleshooting as to how to improve things, we will always see the answer according to the philosophies we hold to.

Two Philosophies of Worship—Table B

If worship is our goal, these are the usual ideas we have for improvement in our worship experience.	If the presence of God is our goal, these are the usual ideas we have for improvement in our worship experience.
We need more rehearsal.	We need more prayer time together.
We need better musicians.	We need worshipers who usher in the presence of God with their instruments.
We need talented or skilled singers.	We need singers who sing prophetically, representing God's heart.
We need an excellent musical ensemble sound, which will attract people from all walks of society to our church.	We need the spirit of unity in our team, which will please the Lord and cause Him to command the blessing in our midst, so there will be nothing impossible to us.
We need to feature only our "first string" worship leaders, who have honed their musical skill and craft.	We need to use people who know the presence of God, trusting God to improve their musical talent and skill.

Table 13

Is it wrong to rehearse or seek out talented and skilled musicians to lead us into corporate worship? Of course it isn't wrong. The ideal is to have both sides of the above chart at work in everyone involved in our local church's worship leadership. However, that would be the ideal, which is seldom (if ever) realized in true life, because we need people to minister as they develop and grow. If we wait until people are fully developed in both their natural and spiritual gifts before we use them on our worship teams or in ministry, we will have very few people ministering and giving worship leadership, if any at all. We will discuss these two philosophies of worship more in-depth throughout the Worship College curriculum.

Since we have taken the time in this chapter to prove biblically which philosophy of worship we are to follow, it is important for us to adopt this philosophy in our individual worship so it will carry over into our corporate worship experiences. Remember, worship is not an end or goal; worship is the means to the goal of experiencing the presence of God so we can know God. Therefore, we need to judge our corporate worship experiences according to this worship philosophy.

Two Philosophies of Worship–Table C

If worship is our goal:	If the presence of God is our goal:
We judge according to the natural quality of our music.	We judge according to the spiritual visitation of God.

Table 14

If worship is our goal, we will do all that we can do to make the expressing of our worship as excellent as we possibly can. However, if the presence of God is our goal and we truly hunger for God's presence out of desperation, the quality of our offering, or expression of worship, has no bearing on reaching our goal. The most important point of leadership judgment, then, becomes the anointing on a person to usher in the presence of God, not his or her musical talent or skill level.

Am I saying that we are not supposed to strive for excellence in the offering we give to God? Of course not! We want to give God the very best offering possible, just as Moses commanded the children of Israel to sacrifice a lamb without spot. What we are saying, however, is that God is not offended by the occasional wrong note or missed timing, because God is looking on and is more interested in the heart of man. Since worship is supposed to be for God, not man, His is the only opinion that counts here.

It is true that the more often we taste of the presence of God, the more we will desire to bring an offering to Him without spot or blemish. However, we must remember that God delights in using the base things of this world to confound the wise. If we are skilled musicians, why do we then need God to give us what we offer unto Him?

Being good musically does not at all guarantee us that we will experience God's presence. However, being anointed to usher in the presence of God, no matter how bad we sound musically, still gets us to the goal of where God wants us to go in our worship.

If you offer me my choice between a talented musician who is anointed to usher in the presence of God and an unskilled musician who also is anointed to usher in the presence of God, I would choose the unskilled one for my worship team. It is my opinion that God gets more glory out of using an ordinary person to usher in His presence than He gets when a talented person ushers in God's presence. The reason for this is the onlookers can't help but notice the developed skill of a trained musician, which makes God have to share glory with that musician. If a talented musician is anointed to usher in the presence of God and he knows how to appear invisible to the onlookers, he would be my first choice. These people are very few and far between, however.

If we make worship our goal, we will judge our worship times according to the flesh. However, if we make the presence of God our goal, God will make sure our musical skill level improves as well. It won't matter to us, then; we will be judging our worship by the goal of God's presence, not by the means God has given us to experience His presence, which is our worship.

Chapter Seven

Rejoice Always—A Study of When to Worship

Rejoice Is a Synonym for Worship

Joy is an emotion—a way we feel. The closest emotion to it would be happiness. However, joy is indeed different from happiness, which we see when we examine them both with an eye for nuance.

Joy can also be a verb of action. To joy in or over a situation, event, or person is to show outward evidence of this inward emotion.

Our attitude or demeanor can be referred to as joyful, full of joy, joyous, etc. Yet, to willfully express joy is to *rejoice*.

In chapter three of this book, we told you there are many words in the Bible which mean to praise or worship almighty God. We indicated that *rejoice* is one of these synonyms. However, we also told you that even synonyms can have slightly different meanings. We began examining these differences in our last chapter about the presence of God when we looked at the nuances regarding thanksgiving, praise, and worship when approaching the presence of God.

In this chapter, we will look at some of the distinctions of the worship synonym *rejoice*. Although in the general sense, *rejoice* means simply "to glorify God," we will examine this word a little more closely.

Worship Is Easy When Life Is Good

No Christian has trouble praising God when everything is going right. When we are joyful and our emotions register high on our "joy meter," praise and thanksgiving simply ooze from us without much effort at all.

It is when life turns challenging that we no longer feel like expressing joy. Does God expect us to worship Him in these times as well as the good times? The answer to this question is definitely *yes!*

> "*Rejoice always, pray without ceasing, in everything give thanks; for this is the will of God in Christ Jesus for you.*" *(1 Thessalonians 5:16–18, NKJV).*

This is one of those Scriptures which is written as a command, not a suggestion. We need to always keep in mind that when God commands us to do something, it is for our good, not His. If we defy His commands, we will be the ones who suffer.

The first command here is two words: "Rejoice always!" There is no question about what God meant by this command. It means we are to always rejoice—no matter what the circumstances or how we feel.

The second command is for us to pray without stopping. God knows there will be times in our lives that will make it difficult for us to talk to Him. Yet, it is at those times we need to keep the communication with God going even more. Therefore, God commanded us to always continue communicating with Him, no matter what is happening in our lives.

Thirdly, we are commanded to give thanks and worship God in every situation we find ourselves. Just in case we think this is an option, Paul makes it clear here that this is God's will for us—to worship God no matter what is going on in our lives.

Our tendency as human beings is to rejoice when life is good and not rejoice when life is a challenge. That is not God's will at all. God wants us to praise Him no matter what is going on in our lives.

Why Do We Suffer?

This age-old philosophical question has been debated for hundreds of years. On one side of this issue, we have those who state that God could not be a good God and allow such suffering to go on in our world.

The Bible makes it clear that God does not cause any suffering! Suffering is the result of mankind's sin. We live in a cursed world. It was cursed as a result of Adam and Eve's sin.

> "Then to Adam He said, "Because you have heeded the voice of your wife, and have eaten from the tree of which I commanded you, saying, 'You shall not eat of it': "Cursed is the ground for your sake." (Genesis 3:17, NKJV).

Because of this curse, we who live here on planet Earth can expect suffering and trouble as long as we are here. Even Jesus tried to warn us about this and encourage us with these words:

> "These things I have spoken to you, that in Me you may have peace. In the world you will have tribulation; but be of good cheer, I have overcome the world." (John 16:33, NKJV).

To live in a cursed world means we all will have difficulties. There is no escaping that fact. However, as Christians, we can overcome the world, since Jesus overcame the world first. We, then, do not have to become depressed or remain in despair. We can rejoice in the knowledge that no matter what we are going through on this earth, it is only temporary. That makes it possible for us to rejoice in the good and in the bad.

Job's Struggles

There are several people in the Bible who have experienced difficulties on the earth; yet, they maintained lifestyles of praise and thanksgiving. One of the most famous ones is Job. He, as you recall, lost everything in one day, including the lives of all his children. Here's how Job dealt with this crushing news.

> "Then Job arose, tore his robe, and shaved his head; and he fell to the ground and worshiped. And he said: Naked I came from my mother's womb, and naked shall I return there. The Lord gave, and the Lord has taken away; blessed be the name of the Lord." In all this Job did not sin nor charge God with wrong." (Job 1:20–22, NKJV).

From the commentary of the writer of the book of Job, we understand without question what is going on inside Job's heart. After receiving such devastating news, Job rose up and did the things his culture taught him to do in a time like that. He tore his clothes and shaved his head. The next thing that happened, Job did not learn from his culture. He learned it from his close relationship with God—Job "worshiped." We know Job had a close relationship with God, because the writer of the book of Job told us he did.

Very seldom will we worship in difficult times by making a decision to worship when the difficulties happen. Our decision to worship God in all things must come before any difficulties show up. Job had made the decision that no matter what happened in his life, he would always praise the Lord.

Here's how Job worshiped in his difficult circumstances: *"The Lord gave, and the Lord has taken away." (Job 1:21, NKJV).*

Without being told that Job was worshiping here, we could misconstrue that Job was blaming these tragedies on God. Many of us do this when we go through hard times. Job was not blaming God for his terrible predicament; Job was attributing to God what Satan had actually done. Job did not have an attitude of anger toward God, because these were the very next words out of Job's mouth: *"Blessed be the name of the Lord." (Job 1:21, NKJV).*

This was not sarcasm; this was true worship. This statement indicates Job's total trust in God, regardless of what had just happened. Oh, that we might learn to trust God with our lives that much!

Just in case we did not understand the purity of worship being expressed here by Job, the author added this phrase of commentary: *"In all this Job did not sin nor charge God with wrong." (Job 1:22, NKJV).*

This makes it clear that Job was not accusing God of evil toward him. Job was simply attributing everything that happened in his life to being under God's control. Did God cause Job to lose everything in one day? Absolutely not! We know, by reading the first part of the story, that it was Satan who did all those things to Job, not God.

But Job said God did it. Can you imagine how angry Satan must have gotten when Job did not give him any credit for all the destruction Satan had done? Job attributed all to God and then blessed Him for it. I personally believe that Satan really likes getting credit for life's devastations. One thing is for sure—when we are angry at the devil, we are not expressing joy to Jesus.

Habakkuk's Struggles

A lesser-known man of God who learned the importance of worshiping God in all things is Habakkuk.

> "Though the fig tree may not blossom, nor fruit be on the vines; though the labor of the olive may fail, and the fields yield no food; though the flock may be cut off from the fold, and there be no herd in the stalls – Yet I will rejoice in the LORD, I will joy in the God of my salvation. The LORD God is my strength; He will make my feet like deer's feet, and He will make me walk on my high hills. To the Chief Musician. With my stringed instruments." (Habakkuk 3:17–19, NKJV).

Let's take a closer look at what was going on in Habakkuk's life. Perhaps you may be able to relate to him in his struggles.

The first problem Habakkuk reported was that...

"the fig tree may not blossom."

Fig trees were a common sight in the Middle East in Bible times. You may remember the story of Jesus cursing the fig tree because it did not have any fruit (Matthew 21:18–22).

Before any fruit tree produces fruit, it blossoms. The flowers on the fruit tree are the promise that fruit will be coming in the process of time. Habakkuk's fig tree did not have any blossoms that year, so there was absolutely no prospect of having figs.

Maybe there is something you have depended on year after year, but this year, even the possibility of it has been removed. If so, you know how Habakkuk felt.

The second problem Habakkuk mentioned was...

"nor fruit be on the vines."

The vine produced grapes—a very important product in the Middle East. In this case, there had been a promise of fruit in the form of blossoms, but the promise was unfulfilled. This can represent promises or dreams we have had in the past that have not come true. The emotions associated with this type of disappointment run very deep and are very hurtful.

The third condition of life Habakkuk found himself in was that…

"the labor of the olive may fail."

Habakkuk was talking about the labor of the olive here, not the olives themselves. When you "work" olives, you extract the oil from them. This oil was thought to have great medicinal applications in Bible times. You may recall the story of the Good Samaritan, who found a man on the road who had been beaten and robbed. To treat this man's wounds, the Samaritan used wine as a disinfectant and oil as a healing agent.

> *"But a certain Samaritan, as he journeyed, came where he was: and when he saw him, he had compassion on him, and went to him, and bound up his wounds, pouring in oil and wine." (Luke 10:33–34, KJV).*

We also see oil associated with supernatural healing in the Bible.

> *"Is anyone among you sick? Let him call for the elders of the church, and let them pray over him, anointing him with oil in the name of the Lord. And the prayer of faith will save the sick, and the Lord will raise him up." (James 5:14–15, NKJV).*

Therefore, I believe what Habakkuk was talking about here was health issues—problems so bad that the treatments (and possibly the prayers) were not making any difference; the oil of the olive failed.

The fourth condition Habakkuk found himself in was that…

"the fields yield no food."

Every farmer knows that growing and harvesting a crop is not an easy task. First, you have to prepare the ground for the seed. Next, you have to plant the seed. If you are irrigating the crop, this needs to be done on a regular basis. Fertilizer must be applied when appropriate. Then comes the harvesting of the crop and safe storage of the grain. All this constitutes a lot of hard work, and—at times—a lot of long hours.

After all his hard work, Habakkuk ended up with no increase or benefit at all. The level of frustration when expected provision does not materialize is intensely frustrating.

The fifth condition Habakkuk expressed was this dilemma...

"the flock may be cut off from the fold."

The flock, in this case, can be thought of as relationships between people. The fold can be thought of as a place of safety, a place where you feel comfortable, or a place where you belong. Perhaps you know what it feels like to be cut off from family or friends. Maybe you know what happened; maybe you don't. Loneliness can be a constant battle to someone in this type of situation.

The sixth condition Habakkuk reported is this:

"there be no herd in the stalls."

In the days that Habakkuk lived, there were no banks where money was kept. People measured wealth by the flocks and herds one owned. In today's world, this statement would be equated to there being no money in the bank. This means there are no resources to fall back on. Everything else which Habakkuk listed is hard, yet tolerable as long as a person has something to fall back on. But when that is gone, that person has really reached the bottom.

Here is a review of all the conditions facing Habakkuk.

Habakkuk's Condition

the fig tree may not blossom	no promise of fruit
nor fruit be on the vines	unrealized promises or dreams
the labor of the olive may fail	health issues
the fields yield no food	expected provision does not materialize
the flock may be cut off from the fold	relationship problems
there be no herd in the stalls	no money in the bank—no reserves

Table 15

Habakkuk's Resolve

It is very difficult—if not impossible—to make a decision to worship God when you are going through difficult times. This decision needs to be made before we experience tribulations so that when we find ourselves in hard places, we simply do what we have already decided to do, which is to worship God.

However, even when we have made a decision ahead of time to give thanks in all things, we can find ourselves in a struggle to honor that decision when the heat is on. That's why we need something stronger than a simple decision to worship God in our trials. We need resolve or conviction in our hearts that, no matter what happens in our lives, we will give God praise.

Resolve is the root word of *resolution*. Do you remember those New Year's resolutions that everyone does not keep? That is not the true meaning of the word *resolve*. A true resolve means you would die before you would break your resolve.

A resolve, in this case, is a determination that, no matter what happens, we will worship God! Here was Habakkuk's resolve:

> "Yet I will rejoice in the LORD, I will joy in the God of my salvation."

What Does it Truly Mean to Rejoice?

To understand a word in the Bible, we must look into the original language and find out the original meaning. When Habakkuk resolved in his heart that he would "rejoice in the Lord" in hard times, it went well beyond what you and I first might think it means. Here is the *Strong's Concordance* definition of this word *rejoice* found in Habakkuk 3:18.

> **rejoice:** 5937 ʻalaz (aw-laz'); a primitive root; to jump for joy, i.e. exult: be joyful, rejoice, triumph.

I looked up *exult* in the *Webster's New World Dictionary* (1979), and here's what I found.

exult: to leap, to rejoice greatly, be jubilant, glory

To rejoice God's way is to express joy so demonstratively that our feet do not stay on the ground. Even the synonym for *rejoice, exult,* carries this same meaning of extreme leaping and dancing, which is a demonstrative style of expressing joy.

Habakkuk is saying, "Even though my world is falling apart, I have resolved to praise my God with leaping and dancing." He also goes on to say, "*I will joy in the God of my salvation.*" (*Habakkuk 3:18, NKJV*) This is a case where *joy* is being used as a verb. Here is the Strong's definition of the word *joy* in this Scripture.

joy: 1523 a primitive root; to spin round (under the influence of any violent emotion), i.e. usually rejoice, or (as cringing) fear: KJV-- be glad, joy, be joyful, rejoice.

Again, we see the demonstration of extreme emotions being expressed by another dance move—to twirl or spin. Habakkuk's resolve to rejoice or joy in the Lord in his hard times was not just to say "praise the Lord" several times. It was to leap, jump, and spin about. His resolve was to dance with all his might before the Lord! By the way, this is impossible to do when you are holding on to depression or despair.

The worse our circumstances, the more demonstrative our rejoicing should be in the Lord. Extreme hardship in our lives should result in extreme rejoicing in our Lord and Savior, Jesus Christ.

Why Dancing?

It takes something extreme to break the effects happening throughout our beings when we experience extreme devastation. When we go through anything in life on the level that Job and Habakkuk did, we must choose to rejoice in the biblical sense—to break ourselves out of depression, even though this depression is a legitimate, natural response to our circumstances.

It is a scientifically proven fact that extreme physical activity releases endorphins into the bloodstream, and these chemicals actually change the way we feel, no matter what our circumstances. When we feel better physically, we are more able to experience hope and faith in our souls and spirits.

Dancing with all our might before the Lord has been lost to the mainstream of Christendom through the centuries. I wonder if that has anything to do with the trend of increased mental illness we see among Christians. Choosing to not worship God in the middle of our trials could drive anybody crazy. What God has told us to do is always for our own good—to help us overcome this world we live in and its effects on us.

God Dances

Where did exuberant dancing originate? God, the creator of everything, is our example of expressing joy in the dance. Read this Scripture with the biblical understanding of the meanings of the words *rejoice* and *joy*:

> "The LORD thy God in the midst of thee is mighty; He will save, He will **rejoice** over thee with joy; He will rest in His love, He will **joy** over thee with singing." (Zephaniah 3:17, KJV).

The word *rejoice* in this Scripture is Strong's Hebrew word number 7797, with a slightly different meaning than number 5937, defined above.

> **rejoice: 7797 suws (soos); or siys (sece);** a primitive root; to be bright, i.e. cheerful: KJV-- be glad, rejoice greatly, joy, make mirth, rejoice.

The first use of the word *joy* in this Scripture is Strong's number 8057. Again, its meaning differs slightly from number 1523, described above.

> joy: **8057 simchah** (sim-khaw'); from 8056;
> blithesomeness or glee, (religious or festival):
> KJV-- joy exceeding (-ly), gladness, joy (-fulness),
> mirth, pleasure, rejoice (-ing).

Both of these words carry the sense of extreme expression of gladness, although their definitions do not identify what extreme expressions are being done. However, the last use of the word *joy* in this Scripture is the same word used in Habakkuk. It is Strong's number 1523, described earlier, which means "to spin about or dance violently."

God dances and sings over us in an extreme manner. This is an incredible realization.

Jesus Danced

Not only do we read about God dancing over us in the Old Testament, but we also read in the New Testament that Jesus danced.

> "In that hour Jesus **rejoiced** in spirit, and said, I thank thee,
> O Father, Lord of heaven and earth." (Luke 10:21, KJV).

The meaning of this Greek word for *rejoice* seems to combine the meanings of all the Hebrew words we studied from the Old Testament. Here is the definition.

> rejoiced: **21 agalliao** (ag-al-lee-ah'-o); from agan
> (much) and 242; properly, to jump for joy,
> i.e. exult: KJV-- be (exceeding) glad, with
> exceeding joy, rejoice (greatly).

Jesus danced, according to this Scripture (see the definition of *exult*). Jesus expressed extreme, great emotions as He rejoiced after His disciples returned from a field trip He sent them on. That was the trip from which they came back excited that even the devils were subject to them in the name of Jesus. Then Jesus told them he was in heaven when Satan was cast out, and He fell to earth like lightening. After Jesus told them about that, He danced and rejoiced greatly.

We can look at this experience in two different ways. First of all, Jesus was rejoicing over the fact that Satan had been cast out of heaven. Secondly, Jesus knew the only way for us to overcome Satan starts with exuberant praise of almighty God.

Whatever His reason—and whatever our circumstances —we should be able to rejoice like Jesus did. I believe this is what He meant when He told us to *"be of good cheer, I have overcome the world."* (*John 16:33, KJV*). By rejoicing in the dance, Jesus demonstrated for us how we, too, can overcome the evil one.

A Result of Exuberant, Extreme Rejoicing

Returning to Habakkuk's experience, the Scripture we read in Habakkuk 3:17–19 revealed to us four results that take place when we rejoice with exuberance and dancing before the Lord in the middle of bad experiences. The first result Habakkuk mentioned is this:

> *"The LORD God is my strength."* (*Habakkuk 3:19, NKJV*).

Depression and despair rob us of any strength we may have. When bad things happen to us, our joy is stolen, making it almost impossible to rejoice. I expect that every one of us have known the truth of this statement by experience. If you haven't experienced this yet, just wait, it will happen—no matter who you are.

If I hadn't seen this next example with my own eyes, I would not share it with you. The controversial practice I am speaking of in this story is called Applied Kinesiology. It is different from the scientific study called Kinesiology, which is endorsed by the medical profession. I leave the research to you to find out why this is controversial among the mainstream medical practitioners, yet is highly used by chiropractors and naturopaths.

Wikipedia gives this definition: "Applied Kinesiology is a system that evaluates structural, chemical, and mental aspects of health using manual muscle testing alongside conventional diagnostic methods." Here's how I have seen it work.

When we lived in Prince George, British Columbia, Canada, we invited two couples from our church to our home for supper. While we were busy getting the meal ready, I was trying to listen in on the conversation between the two men.

"Well, you know," John asserted, "that processed sugar is poison to the human body, don't you?"

"No," Lloyd answered, "I hadn't heard that."

"It is, and I can prove it too," John continued. "Chris, do you have any sugar?" John burst into the kitchen.

"Right here," my wife said as she handed the sugar bowl to John. Curious as to what was going on, we all followed him back to the living room.

"Stand up, Lloyd," John ordered.

Lloyd was at least six foot three and seemed to tower over the five-foot-something friend. John was a salesman for Sears in Prince George and did not engage in a great deal of physical activity. Lloyd, on the other hand, worked on the receiving dock of Sears and was constantly lifting heavy appliances, furniture, and other heavy boxes. Plus, John seemed to be twenty years Lloyd's senior.

"Hold out your hand," John instructed as he reached for Lloyd's right arm and positioned it straight and parallel to the floor, sticking it out beside his body. "I'm going to push down on your arm as hard as I can," John instructed, "and I want you to resist."

"Okay," Lloyd responded, and he prepared for the struggle.

John pulled down with one of his hands with all his might; yet Lloyd's arm remained unmovable. John grabbed his arm with both hands, pulling as hard as he could; still, there was no movement in Lloyd's arm. Finally, John lifted both feet off the ground and hung from Lloyd's arm. Still, there was no noticeable give in the big man's strength.

Setting his feet down on the floor, John began to explain, "Now, our bodies know what is good and bad for us," he began. "If something is good for us, our bodies maintain strength. If we are exposed to something that is bad for us," John continued, "our bodies suddenly become weakened."

"I don't believe that," Lloyd cut in.

"It doesn't matter if you believe it or not," said John. "It is still true. Here, place this spoonful of sugar in your mouth," John said, handing Lloyd a heaping teaspoon of granulated sugar. "Don't swallow it, because it's poison." John qualified his instructions. "Just hold it in your mouth."

Lloyd did as he was requested, because John was a good friend.

"Now," John continued, "I'm going to do the same thing I did before, and I want you to resist me—just like before."

Lloyd stuck his right arm straight out to the side of his body and prepared for the struggle again. This time, John used only three fingers from his left hand—the weaker of his hands—and almost effortlessly pushed Lloyd's right arm down to his side. None of us could believe it, and the one who was most surprised was Lloyd himself.

"I can't believe that," Lloyd shouted with his mouth full of sugar. "Here, try that again," he said, sticking his arm out to his side.

"Sure," John said, and with one finger, he pushed Lloyd's arm straight down to his side. "Now, go spit out the sugar," John calmly said, "and rinse your mouth out real good, and we'll try it again."

When Lloyd returned from the bathroom, he assumed the position as he had before, with his right arm out to his side. John tried again to pull Lloyd's arm down, and he had to use two hands to get it to dip two inches.

"The reason you are not as strong as you were before," John explained, "is because your body has absorbed some of the sugar through the tissue in your mouth."

"That's amazing," Lloyd sighed as he sat back down on the chesterfield.

I wouldn't believe it if I hadn't seen it for myself. Of course, since that first exposure to Applied Kinesiology, I have come across many other applications of its use. It never ceases to amaze me how quickly our physical strength can change when exposed to this type of test.

One person did the same type of strength test by having their innocent volunteers think happy thoughts. While thinking these thoughts, their arm strength was very strong. Next, they were instructed to think anything negative. They were given some examples, like a bill they needed to pay, a relationship gone bad, or whatever caused them the most fear. Every person who honestly cooperated with this test became weak, to varying degrees, while thinking negative thoughts. This test has also proven consistently that every person who thought the phrase *Jesus is Lord* over his or her previous negative thought proved to become physically stronger than when he or she simply thought the happy thought.

God has set the world up to function in this way, and He has tried to get us to reap the benefits of His strength in us by commanding us to "rejoice always!" The Bible makes it clear to us that joy will be our strength.

> "Then he said unto them, Go your way, eat the fat, and drink the sweet, and send portions unto them for whom nothing is prepared: for this day is holy unto our Lord: neither be ye sorry; for the **joy** of the LORD is your **strength**" (Nehemiah 8:10, KJV).

> "In His neck remaineth **strength**, and sorrow is turned into **joy** before Him." (Job 41:22, KJV).

We see that the first result of rejoicing before the Lord in the dance will be for us to be strengthened to face whatever we are facing with God's strength. This is reason enough to obey God's command to rejoice always!

Other Results of Biblical Rejoicing

Habakkuk's second result of rejoicing before the Lord is that...

> "He will make my feet like deer's feet." (Habakkuk 3:19, NKJV).

What is the mystery of this statement? What could it possibly mean? I am not the first to put forth this exegesis for this Scripture, but I had heard it second-, third-, and fourth-hand from so many different sources—without a shred of documentation to back it up—that I didn't even know if the original premise was factual or not. Therefore, I did my own investigation, and here's what I found.

I looked for a website dedicated to teaching people how to track deer, and I found several. On this page of one such website, http://www.coueswhitetail.com/coues_biology/coues_deer_sign.htm, I found pictures and statements to verify the premise.

The premise I have heard preached from concerning this text is that a deer's back feet will come down in the exact same spot that his front feet have stepped. Now I have seen the documentation to prove that premise.

The application of this premise is this—the Scripture says that when I obey God's command to rejoice always, my feet will become exactly like the back feet of a deer. My feet will follow exactly in the footsteps of my leader, who is Jesus Christ. This speaks of obedience—to follow Jesus wherever He leads.

This makes sense. Once we become obedient to rejoice with jumping, leaping, twirling, and violent dancing, it becomes easier for us to obey and follow Jesus in anything else He wants.

The third result of this type of exuberant worship is that...

"He will make me walk on my high hills." (Habakkuk 3:19, NKJV).

What are your "high hills"? What dreams and hopes has God put within your heart to obtain for Him? What has God called you to achieve in your lifetime? The key to reaching your high hills is to obey God's command to rejoice always!

The fourth result is found in the final statement of this short prophetic book written by Habakkuk:

"To the Chief Musician. With my stringed instruments."

From this phrase, we learn that Habakkuk had just written a song that he was passing along to his chief musician. The first chief musician in the Bible was appointed by David. This was recorded in 1 Chronicles 15:22. By the very next chapter, that chief musician had retired, and King David had appointed Asaph chief in 1 Chronicles 16:5. Then it tells us in verse 7 that David wrote a song that He delivered to the chief musician, who seemed to have orchestrated and arranged it for the large worship orchestra and choir to play and sing before the people. It is reasonable to assume that Habakkuk had done the very same thing—written a song, then given it to his chief musician for arranging.

To apply this to us today, I believe it is reasonable to assume that one of the results of obeying God's command to rejoice always is God giving us a brand new song of praise to sing.

> "He has put a new song in my mouth—Praise to our God; many will see it and fear, And will trust in the Lord." (Psalm 40:3, NKJV).

This type of obedience to God will result in songs of praise being birthed in us with a new level of creativity.

I would say the benefits which come from obeying God's command to rejoice always far outweigh the pain of personal crucifixion required for us to obey that command. May we never lose sight of the fact that God's commands are for our benefit.

Chapter Eight

Perfected Praise

Make His Praise Glorious

We have seen that it is God's choice to inhabit, or be enthroned, in our praises of Him.

> "But You are holy, Enthroned in the praises of Israel" (Psalm 22:3, NKJV). "But Thou art holy, O Thou that inhabitest the praises of Israel." (Psalm 22:3, KJV).

Knowing that God Himself—the Creator of the universe—chooses to come and dwell in our praise motivates us to make our praises the best they can be for Him.

If I knew that the Queen of England would be visiting my house, I would scrub that place for weeks, preparing for her visit. I would probably be up all night before that day, making sure everything was prepared properly for her fifteen minutes in my home. I doubt that any of you would consider these actions excessive, and many of you would do a whole lot more than me. In the same way we are motivated to put our best foot forward for the Queen, we are also motivated to perfect our praises, which the King of Kings dwells in.

Every time we worship Jesus, He comes and inhabits our praise. Our collective praises become a house for Him to inhabit. Knowing that fact motivates us to want to build Him the best house we can. Even David felt this way.

"Sing out the honor of His name; make His praise glorious."
(Psalm 66:2, NKJV).

But the question is this: what does God mean by glorious or perfected praise, and how does it compare to man's definition?

Man's Natural Definition of Perfected Praise

If worship is our goal, we will address this desire to "make His praise glorious" from a natural perspective. This means we will concentrate all our efforts on improving the presentation of our worship.

The mainstream of Christendom hires professional singers and organists to lead its worship, supplementing large ensembles with only skilled volunteers. The contemporary churches may not pay money for the services of their musicians, but they do provide an atmosphere in which their musicians can enjoy recognition for their musical skills. Recognition is worth more to some than money. For a further discussion on this topic, I refer you back to chapter two of this book.

If worship is our goal, we judge our worship according to our natural abilities and natural understanding of what it means to perfect our praise. Secular musical training has taught us to compete with other instrumentalists and singers for the concertmaster position, for first chair in our section of band or orchestra, or for the role of section leader in our choral section. We see this spirit of competition as a healthy thing which motivates everyone to continue to better themselves and their musical skills.

Many churches adopt the philosophy that only the newest and most popular songs are what should be used for worship. If your church is large enough, your leadership may develop a sports-team-like approach to who is used to lead worship—first string worship leaders on Sunday morning, second string on Sunday night, and third string for midweek gatherings. This insures that the best musicians the church has are being used to lead worship at the most-attended service.

What I am describing may be the criteria your church uses to determine who leads worship and what songs are used in worship. I have told you that every one of us will naturally want to offer our King the best praise possible. That seems commendable; however, this approach is the natural way of thinking, which is not the way God thinks.

God's Definition of Perfected Praise

If the presence of God is our goal, not worship, we will be able to discover and embrace God's definition for perfected praise. God judges everything from a completely different perspective than what man does.

> "Do ye look on things after the outward appearance?" (2 Corinthians 10:7, KJV)

> "But the Lord said to Samuel, 'Do not look at his appearance or at his physical stature, because I have refused him. For the Lord does not see as man sees; for man looks at the outward appearance, but the Lord looks at the heart.'" (1 Samuel 16:7, NKJV).

This is a fact—we, as human beings, will always look at a situation from a natural viewpoint. God will always look at things from a spiritual viewpoint. Our prayer is that God would help us see things from His perspective.

How does God define "perfected praise"?

There is only one place in the entire Bible that the phrase *perfected praise* appears.

> "Then the blind and the lame came to Him in the temple, and He healed them. But when the chief priests and scribes saw the wonderful things that He did, and the children crying out in the temple and saying, "Hosanna to the Son of David!" they were indignant and said to Him, "Do You hear what these are saying?"
>
> "And Jesus said to them, "Yes. Have you never read, 'Out of the mouth of babes and nursing infants You have **perfected praise**'?" (Matthew 21:14–16, NKJV)

Jesus said that perfected praise comes from young children. Well, that is certainly a different way to look at this whole situation. By embracing this one revelation, our perspective of perfected praise is completely destroyed.

> ➤ Perfected praise cannot mean to use only the most highly skilled instrumentalists and singers. Young children have not lived long enough to perfect their musical skills. Science tells us that in order to distinguish yourself in any area, such as music or sports, you are required to spend an average of ten thousand hours working on that skill.

> ➤ Perfected praise cannot mean to only use the newest published songs. Children do not have the resources to accomplish that. Besides, I have heard children sing the same old song over and over and never tire of it.

> ➤ Perfected praise cannot mean to depend on a spirit of competition to improve the musical skills of all involved. Any time I have seen the spirit of competition encouraged for a group of children, it has always turned into a very negative experience for all involved.

> ➤ Perfected praise cannot mean to pay for the best singers and instrumentalists. Children don't relate to the monetary system of the adult world. They need no money or recognition to sing from their hearts.

> ➤ Perfected praise cannot mean to perfect the presentation of our worship. These children had no rehearsal at all. Their worship was spontaneous. All children are at varying stages of the pitch-matching process. This means that they sing off-key as much as they sing on pitch. Singing the right notes is not a criterion for perfected praise.

The Setting of Perfected Praise

Earlier that morning, Jesus had entered Jerusalem riding on a colt. The large crowd around Jesus paved His entrance into the city with their clothes and tree branches. As He entered the city, the crowd shouted.

"Then the multitudes who went before and those who followed cried out, saying: 'Hosanna to the Son of David! "Blessed is He who comes in the name of the Lord!" Hosanna in the highest!"" (Matthew 21:9, NKJV)

You would think that when the large crowd declared Jesus to be the Son of David, they understood they were declaring Jesus to be the Messiah of promise, the Lord's Christ. Whereas some in the crowd may have understood that, most of them did not. When the people in the city asked the crowd who was entering the city that day, they answered like this:

"So the multitudes said, 'This is Jesus, the prophet from Nazareth of Galilee.'" (Matthew 21:11, NKJV).

There is a big difference between being a prophet and being the Christ. Therefore, we understand that most of the people in this multitude welcoming Jesus into Jerusalem that day were not convinced that Jesus was the Christ—otherwise they would not simply call Him a prophet. They also would not have turned on Jesus at the end of that week by calling for His crucifixion.

The first stop Jesus made that morning, after entering the city, was at the temple. Upon entering the temple, Jesus angrily overturned the tables of the money changers and those who bought and sold. This act of cleansing the temple speaks to us today about purifying our hearts' motives before we worship.

You would think that the crowd would stay clear of someone who demonstrated such public anger, but instead, *"the blind and the lame came to Him in the temple, and He healed them." (Matthew 21:11, NKJV).* Even angry, Jesus demonstrated such love that those in need knew they could come to Him for help.

Whenever Jesus performed miracles here on earth, He did them for two reasons. First, He was moved by compassion.

"And Jesus went forth, and saw a great multitude, and was moved with compassion toward them, and He healed their sick." (Matthew 14:14, KJV).

Jesus explained the second reason He did miracles in this Scripture.

> "He who has seen Me has seen the Father; so how can you say, 'Show us the Father'? Do you not believe that I am in the Father, and the Father in Me? The words that I speak to you I do not speak on My own authority; but the Father who dwells in Me does the works. Believe Me that I am in the Father and the Father in Me, or else believe Me for the sake of the works themselves." (John 14:9b–11, NKJV).

Summarized, the second reason Jesus did miracles was to reveal who He is by what He does. However, only those who were truly looking for the Christ recognized Him by the works He did.

The Children Who Offered Perfected Praise

Every Jewish child is taught from birth about the promised Messiah—the Redeemer, who is the Christ. One key fact they are taught is that He will come through the line of David's decedents. That is why He would be called the son of David.

Another important thing Jewish children are taught is how to recognize the Christ when He comes. Among other things, they are instructed that one way to recognize the Messiah is by the loving miracles He would do. That's why Jesus told His disciples, "believe Me for the sake of the works themselves." (John 14: 11, NKJV).

The innocence of childhood somehow gets lost when we grow older. Things we found easy to believe as children become more and more difficult to believe as adults. Rationalization, rather than faith, becomes the way we think. Although we know the right things to say to make it sound like we still believe, inside we know that we no longer believe them. Disappointments, hurts, and doubts contribute to our lack of faith.

> "Hope deferred maketh the heart sick: but when the desire cometh, it is a tree of life." (Proverbs 13:23, KJV).

The adults who were alive when Jesus came to earth had waited for generations for their messiah to come, yet had slipped into unbelief somewhere along the line. On the other hand, the children had been to classes recently which told them about the coming Christ—the son of David—and how to recognize Him when He arrived. This information was very fresh in their minds. Their faith was heightened and not tainted by the disappointments of life. They truly expected their Messiah to come at any time.

These conditions remind me somewhat of adult Christians today who know intellectually and doctrinally that Jesus will return to earth for His bride but have ceased to expect it.

When these children recognized who Jesus was by what He did, they got excited like only children can do. When children get excited about something, they get very loud and expel enormous amounts of energy! They are not conscious of the rules of public etiquette. They don't care if they are dignified while expressing their excitement. They will shout at the top of their lungs, squeal, and scream. They will jump up and down, dance and twirl around, fall down, and more, because they are so excited.

We could describe this type of outburst as reckless abandonment from all dignity or proper public behavior. This is what Jesus called "perfected praise."

When these children realized who Jesus was, they began shouting or crying out in the temple and saying, "*Hosanna to the Son of David!*" (*Matthew 21:9, NKJV*) Unlike their adult counterparts who had shouted the exact same thing while Jesus entered the city earlier that day, these children actually believed what they were shouting. They knew they had found the Christ, and they were rejoicing that He had come in their lifetime.

Perfected Praise Summarized

The first requirement to make our praise perfect is that we must believe what we are shouting or singing. Further to this, perfected praise is reckless abandonment in our worship, as demonstrated for us by these noisy children. It is simply losing ourselves in the expression of our love for God. Perfected praise is expressed with a high level of energy. It is extreme worship with no regard for dignity. It is highly intensive praise. Perfected praise is acting like an excited kid while giving glory to Jesus. It is high-volume, high-intensity praise, with nothing held back. This is God's perspective of perfected praise.

Comfortable Life Philosophies

We see that God's way of looking at things is never man's way. To illustrate this further, let's examine some differences concerning other life philosophies.

Two Perspectives on Life

Life Area	Man's Perspective	God's Perspective
finances	conserve your money	"Give, and it shall be given unto you" (Luke 6:38, KJV)
physical strength	conserve your energy	"And whatsoever ye do, do it heartily" (Colossians 3:23, KJV)
survival	conserve your life	"Greater love has no one than this, than to lay down one's life for his friends" (John 15:13, NKJV)

Table 16

God's ideas are extreme; man's ideas are comfortable. Here's what God thinks about our conservative philosophies of life.

> "And to the angel of the church of the Laodiceans write, 'These things says the Amen, the Faithful and True Witness, the Beginning of the Creation of God: "I know your works, that you are neither cold nor hot. I could wish you were cold or hot. So then, because you are lukewarm, and neither cold nor hot, I will vomit you out of My mouth." (Revelation 3:14–16, NKJV).

Conservative worship is not acceptable to God.

God's Greatest Commandment

When a lawyer came to Jesus and ask Him what the greatest commandment is, here is how Jesus responded:

"And thou shalt love the Lord thy God with all thy heart, and with all thy soul, and with all thy mind, and with all thy strength: this is the first commandment." (Mark 12:30, KJV).

We have determined that worship is the expression of mankind's love for Jesus. Therefore, when we worship Him, we are to do so with 100 percent of our beings—not holding back anything. We are to love God with *all* three parts of our person—spirit, soul/mind, and strength (which is our bodies).

These children stumbled into the way God has always wanted to be worshiped with reckless abandonment, nothing held back, loving God with all our beings. For adults to do this, we are required to die to ourselves. This goes against every survival instinct we have awakened. Therefore, this type of praise is hardest to do by the self-aware adult. Children, on the other hand, are not self-aware. They can express their joy without once questioning, "Who is watching me?" This is why Jesus said we must all return to the innocence of childhood to enter and truly understand the kingdom of heaven.

"At that time the disciples came to Jesus, saying, "Who then is greatest in the kingdom of heaven?" Then Jesus called a little child to Him, set him in the midst of them, and said, "Assuredly, I say to you, unless you are converted and become as little children, you will by no means enter the kingdom of heaven. Therefore whoever humbles himself as this little child is the greatest in the kingdom of heaven." (Matthew 18:1–4, NKJV).

Being converted does not require acting as a child—only entering and functioning in the kingdom of heaven. Being a member of the kingdom of heaven is to come into a progressive, loving relationship with the King and to express that love to Him the way He wants us to express it—as ecstatic children.

The Religious Response to Perfected Praise

> What are the seven deadliest words for any church?
> **We've never done it that way before.**

As these little children were shouting at the tops of their lungs, "Hosanna to the Son of David," the religious leaders in the temple that day started to boil with anger. Next, they looked for a way to control these children. I venture to suggest that every one of these scribes and priests had tried to silence those children without success. Their only hope to get these children to be quiet, they thought, was to get Jesus to correct them. If only Jesus would tell the children they were mistaken in thinking that He was the Christ, then the children would shut up.

> *"But when the chief priests and scribes saw the wonderful things that He did, and the children crying out in the temple and saying, "Hosanna to the Son of David!" they were indignant and said to Him, "Do You hear what these are saying?" (Matthew 21:14–15, NKJV)*

"Can you believe what these children are saying?" the religious leaders pleaded. "Isn't it the most ridiculous thing you have heard? Don't you want to tell them to be quiet? I mean, do you hear what they are shouting?"

I love the response Jesus gave to the chief priests and scribes that day. "Yes, I hear," He responded. "What's the matter, haven't you ever read the Scriptures?" Jesus said sarcastically.

The job of the scribes was to copy the Scriptures by hand, over and over, day in and day out. The primary responsibilities of the priests were to read the Scriptures and offer sacrifices. When Jesus asked them, "Have you never read?" it was the most biting, sarcastic put-down anyone could have said to them.

Then Jesus quoted a passage from Psalms 8. *"Out of the mouth of babes and nursing infants You have **perfected praise**."* He was saying, "I am who they are saying I am, so why should I tell them to be quiet?"

Perfected Praise Is Ordained Strength

The only Scripture in the Bible which contains the phrase "perfected praise" is Matthew 21:16—but I just said that Jesus quoted a Scripture from the book of Psalms. If that is true, then there should be two places in the Bible where that phrase appears. Here is the original text of that Scripture in Psalm 8:2, which Jesus quoted.

> "Out of the mouth of babes and nursing infants You have **ordained strength**, because of Your enemies, That You may silence the enemy and the avenger." (NKJV).

Since Jesus is the living Word of God, He is the only one who is allowed to rewrite Scripture. When he does so, we are able to learn something about perfected praise that we would not otherwise know—perfected praise is the same thing as ordained strength. In other words, we receive strength when we praise God with reckless abandonment. When we weary ourselves as we praise the Lord, a miracle occurs. Instead of getting tired, we supernaturally receive strength.

More than once in my life, I have experienced this miracle. I remember dragging myself to church, thinking I would just rest during worship because I was so tired. Yet, when I got there, I began to worship the Lord. Before I knew it, I was giving my all in worship. By the time worship was over, I had been totally renewed and refreshed, and my strength had returned to me.

I have also experienced the opposite of that as well. There have been times when my flesh won the battle and I only worshiped halfheartedly. That's when I experienced greater fatigue leaving the worship service than I had come with.

This is one of those paradoxes we spoke of earlier ("*Give, and it shall be given unto you*"). The natural mind thinks that when you are tired, you should rest. But God says, "If you give every ounce of strength you have when you worship Me, you will supernaturally receive strength."

God has ordained that we receive strength by praising Him—but not with just any type of praise. This strength *only* comes from perfected praise—reckless abandonment in worship. Perfected, extreme praise is the way God has ordained for us to receive strength!

Perfected Praise = **Ordained Strength**

The Reason God Ordained Strength through Extreme Worship

Why does God ordain strength for us when we worship Him in this radical way?

*"Out of the mouth of babes and sucklings hast Thou ordained strength **because of Thine enemies**, that Thou mightest still the enemy and the avenger." (Psalm 8:2, KJV).*

The reason God ordained that we receive strength through radical worship is because God has enemies. God wants to use His people to still or stop His enemies. High-energy praise will give us supernatural strength with which to do this.

Lucifer, God's Enemy

Lucifer is a created being by God, and at one time, he was one of three archangels in heaven.

"You were the anointed cherub who covers; I established you; you were on the holy mountain of God; You walked back and forth in the midst of fiery stones. You were perfect in your ways from the day you were created, Till iniquity was found in you." (Ezekiel 28:14–15, NKJV).

Lucifer's job in heaven—what God anointed him to do—was to cover God's throne and reflect His glory. Some say (and I agree with them) that this was the job of the worship leader of heaven. But Lucifer was not satisfied to facilitate the worship of God in heaven. He wanted worship for himself.

"How you are fallen from heaven, O Lucifer, son of the morning! How you are cut down to the ground, You who weakened the nations! For you have said in your heart:① 'I will ascend into heaven,②I will exalt my throne above the stars of God; ③I will also sit on the mount of the congregation ④On the farthest sides

*of the north; ⑤I will ascend above the heights of the clouds, I
will be like the Most High.'" (Isaiah 14:12–14, NKJV)*

All these five positions are for receiving worship, not leading worship.
It is clear from this Scripture that Lucifer wanted to receive worship to
himself, not lead the worship directed to God. There is also one more
thing Lucifer wanted. *"I will be like the Most High."* Lucifer wanted to be
like God and receive worship for himself.

Lucifer's Punishment

The first part of Lucifer's punishment for his sin was to be expelled
from heaven.

> *"And the seventy returned again with joy, saying, Lord, even
> the devils are subject unto us through Thy name. And He
> said unto them, I beheld Satan as lightning fall from heaven."*
> *(Luke 10:17–18, KJV).*

> *"How you are fallen from heaven, O Lucifer, son of the
> morning! How you are cut down to the ground." (Isaiah
> 14:12–14, NKJV).*

Please notice where God banished Satan to. God exiled Lucifer to
the ground. This Hebrew word [Strong's number 0776] is 'erets (eh'-
rets). This word has been translated in the Old Testament as "land"
1,543 times, as "earth" 712 times, as "ground" ninety-eight times, and as
"world" four times. It is clear that God exiled Lucifer to the earth—the
same planet that He placed mankind on.

Why did God create and place man on the same planet where He
banished Satan? Wouldn't it make more sense to put Lucifer on Jupiter
or the hot planet, Mercury?

Mankind Is Part of Satan's Punishment

Lucifer's first sin—which got him kicked out of heaven—was his
desire to be like God. To punish Satan for this, God chose to create an
entire race of beings in His image.

> "Then God said, 'Let Us make man in Our image, according to Our likeness; let them have dominion ... over all the earth.'" (Genesis 1:26, NKJV).

God put this race of beings made in His own image on the earth where He had banished Lucifer and put them in charge of the entire planet. Man's presence on the earth is to remind Satan that he can never be like the Most High God. Every time Lucifer looks at one of us, he remembers why he lost his place in heaven by desiring something God never intended for him.

The second sin Lucifer committed was to desire to arise to a position where he could also receive worship. That is why God created an entire race of beings whose primary purpose is to worship the Most High God.

> "This people I have formed for Myself; They shall declare My praise." (Isaiah 43:21, NKJV).

Therefore, every time Lucifer looks at a human being, he is reminded that he will never receive worship, and he has lost his chance forever to lead worship in heaven.

Remember, we were created in the image of God with the primary purpose of worshiping God as part of God's plan to punish Lucifer.

High Praises

Let us take just a few moments to review Psalm 149.

> "Praise the Lord! Sing to the Lord a new song, and His praise in the assembly of saints. Let Israel **rejoice** in their Maker; let the children of Zion be **joyful** in their King. Let them praise His name with the **dance**; let them sing praises to Him with the timbrel and harp. For the Lord takes pleasure in His people; He will beautify the humble with salvation." (Psalm 149:1–4, NKJV).

I have set three words in bold text in these verses which all have the synonym *exult*. Do you recall from our studies in chapter seven of this book the meaning of the word *exult*? Let me remind you of it.

exult: to leap, to rejoice greatly, be jubilant, glory

The majority of Psalm 149 is God's commandments for us to worship Him with exuberant, demonstrative praise—with leaping and dancing. This type of extreme praise would qualify as what Jesus called perfected praise.

With this in mind, let's look at the rest of Psalm 149.

"Let the saints be joyful in glory; let them sing aloud on their beds. Let the high praises of God be in their mouth, and a two-edged sword in their hand, to execute vengeance on the nations, and punishments on the peoples; to bind their kings with chains, and their nobles with fetters of iron; to execute on them the written judgment. This honor have all His saints. Praise the Lord!" (Psalm 149:5–9, NKJV)

Psalm 149:5 continues God's instructions to His people for functioning here on earth. It tells us that whenever we are giving God glory, it should be with extreme, radical, perfected praise. This is summarized in God's command for us to be joyful while giving God glory.

The next instruction is for us to sing aloud on our beds. The literal translation of this phrase is to sing loudly while being sexually intimate with your spouse. Those of us who are married realize how inappropriate that would be. The marriage bed is to be a place for beautiful, tasteful, intimate moments. To sing loudly at that time would totally change the moment into something very extreme—but that is the point. Radical, perfected praise is boisterous worship in situations where we would normally be quiet, such as our bed or in the temple, where the normal activities are quiet and reserved.

This next phrase of instruction is the culmination of all the instructions in Psalm 149.

"Let the high praises of God be in their mouth, and a two-edged sword in their hand." (Psalm 149:6, NKJV).

First of all, notice the phrase "high praises." This is the only time this Hebrew word for high appears in the entire Bible. These particular types of praises are distinct from most other praises mentioned in the Bible. From the context of this chapter, there is a sense that high praises imply high energy, high intensity, and extreme praise, even as we defined perfected praise. It is my opinion that these are one and the same.

Perfected Praise = **High Praises**

Hebrew Parallelism

There is a writing technique which the Hebrews—and other cultures in the eastern hemisphere—use all the time called Hebrew parallelism. Our Bible is filled with examples of this literary technique; yet those of us from the western hemisphere of the world do not recognize it, because we don't know what to look for.

A simplified definition of Hebrew parallelism is saying the same thing in two different ways. Here's an obvious example, once you know what you are looking for.

> *"But the Anointing which you have received from Him abides in you, and you do not need that anyone teach you; but as the same Anointing teaches you concerning all things, and* **is true**, *and* **is not a lie**, *and just as It has taught you, you will abide in Him." (1 John 2:27, NKJV).*

Here John is saying that the anointing (which is the Holy Spirit) that we have received from God is true, and is not a lie.

This parallelism was very easy to spot. Let's look at one more example of parallelism in the Bible that you are more familiar with, because it is often quoted concerning worship.

> *"Enter into His gate with thanksgiving, and into His court with praise." (Psalm 100:4, NKJV).*

The western mind will not recognize this as parallelism right away. We have always been taught that this scripture represents a progression in our worship from thanksgiving to praise, therefore we justify the defining of thanksgiving and praise as two different things. To the eastern mind this is obvious parallelism, and validates their belief that thanksgiving and praise are synonyms.

In the west, a court yard is surrounded by the castle or dwelling. We learn that architectural design from the European model. However, in the eastern hemisphere, the European model of a court yard is hardly ever found. They have a completely different concept of a court yard. I learned this from spending time in Viet Nam and Hong Kong, China.

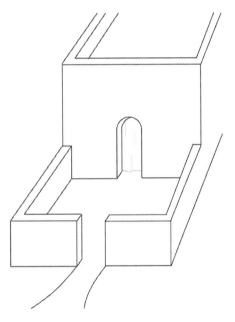

No matter how elaborate an eastern house is, they all are built on this similar design shown in this drawing. The court yard is what we in the west would call our "front yard." Once you enter into their gate you are immediately in their court. To enter their gate is to enter their court. It is the same thing.

In the west we enter someone's gate, then their house. After wandering through their house, we enter their court yard. This is not so in the eastern hemisphere. When you enter the gate, you have entered the court.

This classic Scripture about worship in Psalms 100 is Hebrew parallelism. Therefore, the Psalmist is saying the same thing two different ways.

Parallelism in Psalm 149

Please pay attention to this Hebrew parallelism found in Psalm 149:6. It is very important that we understand this Scripture through this hermeneutical technique.

> "Let the high praises of God be in their mouth, and a two-edged sword in their hand." (Psalm 149:6, NKJV).

High praises in our mouths are the same as spiritual swords in our hands. When we praise God with perfected, extreme, high praises, it is the same thing as having spiritual swords in our hands with which we do damage to God's enemy.

The purpose of a sword is not to look good hanging from your waist. It is not to simply wave above your head to threaten the enemy. The purpose of a sword is to inflict damage upon your enemy. Every time we praise God with all our heart, mind/soul, and strength, that praise cuts and stabs the enemy. Our praise literally does damage to the satanic/demonic forces, who are God's sworn enemies. Worship also binds the strong man, or the higher-ranking demons.

> "To bind their kings with chains, and their nobles with fetters of iron." (Psalm 149:8, NKJV)

God ordered three levels of punishment against Satan and his demons. Let me outline them for you in this chart.

The Three Levels of Satan's Punishment

Level	Punishment	Punishment Explained
1	**Exiled from heaven to planet earth**	Lucifer, who is also called Satan or the devil, was expelled from heaven and banished to the earth.
2	**Constantly Reminded of his sin**	God created a race of people in His image whose primary purpose is to worship God.
3	**Inflicted Pain and Restraint through our worship**	By functioning in our purpose as people, every time we offer high praises to God, we inflict pain on the kingdom of Satan.

Table 17

The Kingdom of Satan

In heaven, before Satan's exile, there was no one closer to God than Lucifer. No one understood as much about God's creation, how God designed things to work, or God's purposes and plans as Lucifer. He was *"the anointed cherub who covers." (Ezekiel 28:14 KJV)*

One of God's ideas Lucifer has adopted in his kingdom here on earth is a chain of command. God had organized the angels in heaven by rank and file. It is suggested that the different names for angels found in the Bible, such as seraphim and cherubim, are not names for different types of angels, but rather, different ranks within the heavenly hosts.

As a matter of fact, Lucifer was one of the highest-ranking angels in heaven before he sinned. He was an archangel and had one-third of the angels in heaven under his command. The other two archangels were Michael and Gabriel, each commanding about one-third of the angels.

Michael is in charge of security. He and his angels are warriors. Gabriel is in charge of communications, among other things. Lucifer was in charge of leading heaven and the universe in worship of almighty God.

I told you that Lucifer was cast out of heaven, but now let me tell you how that event transpired.

> *"And there was war in heaven: Michael and his angels fought against the dragon; and the dragon fought and his angels, and prevailed not; neither was their place found any more in heaven. And the great dragon was cast out, that old serpent, called the Devil, and Satan, which deceiveth the whole world: he was cast out into the earth, and his angels were cast out with him." (Revelation 12:7–9, KJV).*

Since being exiled to earth, Satan has taken this godly concept of chain of command and used it to organize his own kingdom here on earth. Paul the apostle knew and understood this, and he wrote about it in his letter to the Ephesians.

> *"For we do not wrestle against flesh and blood, but against principalities, against powers, against the rulers of the darkness of this age, against spiritual hosts of wickedness in the heavenly places. Therefore take up the whole armor of*

God, that you may be able to withstand in the evil day, and having done all, to stand." (Ephesians 6:12–13, NKJV).

Paul explains here that, in the demonic kingdom of Satan, there is rank and file. He identified four different ranks of demons. Let me list them here, starting with the highest rank first.

4. *"wickedness in the heavenly places"*
3. *"rulers of the darkness"*
2. *"powers"*
1. *"principalities"*

From this, we understand that the human race must contend with more than Satan himself here on the earth. There are millions of demons exiled here on the earth. That wouldn't be so bad if they all were fighting themselves as well as us, vying for position and rank—but they're not. Satan knows firsthand how rebellion in the ranks can weaken effectiveness. Therefore, Satan maintains strict discipline in his ranks. In other words, God's enemy—who is also our enemy—is very well organized.

To Execute Punishments

We have been put on this earth to carry out God's punishment on the devil and his angels. When we worship God wholeheartedly, we inflict extreme pain on the devil and all his demons. High praises are the same thing as having spiritual swords in our hands and using them skillfully.

> *"Let the high praises of God be in their mouth, and a two-edged sword in their hand, to execute vengeance on the nations, and punishments on the peoples; to bind their kings with chains, and their nobles with fetters of iron; to execute on them the written judgment. This honor have all His saints. Praise the Lord!" (Psalm 149:6–9, NKJV)*

What exactly are we suppose to do with this sword of worship? God tells us in this Scripture:

➢ *"execute vengeance"*
➢ *"and punishments"*
➢ *"to bind with chains"*
➢ *"to bind with fetters of iron"*
➢ *"to execute the written judgment"*

Let this sink into your mind. We can do all of this with worship. While we are giving God our love—while we are holding nothing back as we praise Him—His (and our) enemies are being punished. If we do not praise God the way He wants to be praised, none of this will happen. God will not have His vengeance. The kingdom of Satan will not be punished for their crimes against heaven. Demons and the devil will have the freedom to move about the earth and attack the saints of God and innocent people. The written judgments which God, the righteous judge, has issued from His throne will not be carried out.

In this Scripture, we are told who is to have these punishments executed on them. There are four categories of individuals listed:

1. *"the nations"*
2. *"the peoples"*
3. *"kings"*
4. *"nobles"*

Throughout the Bible, references are made to demonic forces as though the demons are human beings. One place this is done is in the book of Daniel. He was fasting and asking God some specific questions. Daniel fasted for three weeks without an answer from God. Finally, on the twenty-fourth day, Gabriel showed up with the answers Daniel was waiting for. Gabriel told Daniel that on the first day Daniel began to ask God for his answers, God had sent Gabriel to him. But when Gabriel reached the air space over Persia, the Prince of Persia fought Gabriel and kept him from reaching Daniel. God finally had to send Michael, the warrior archangel, to fight for Gabriel so he could carry out his mission.

Although there was a human counterpart in Persia called the Prince of Persia, he was not the individual who kept Gabriel from reaching Daniel. It was a ruler of darkness in the heavenly realm who resisted Gabriel.

These types of stories are duplicated throughout the Bible. Therefore, when Psalm 149 says we are to execute vengeance and punishments against people and their leaders, it is talking about the demonic chain of command. Notice how these two lists from Psalm 149 and Ephesians 6 overlay and match up.

Demonic Chain of Command

Rank	Ephesians 6	Psalm 149
1	principalities	the nations
2	powers	the peoples
3	rulers of the darkness	kings
4	wickedness in the heavenly places	nobles

Table 18

The Written Judgment

In every court of law, there is a court recorder who transcribes everything being said as a matter of record. The most important parts of that transcript are the judgment of the court and the sentence of the court. God has held court for Lucifer, passed judgment, and issued the sentence or punishment for Lucifer's crimes. For this trial, Isaiah served as the court recorder and wrote down every punishment God declared that Lucifer will suffer throughout the ages. Would you like to read God's sentence of punishment for Lucifer? Here it is in its entirety.

> "The Lord has broken the staff of the wicked, The scepter of the rulers; He who struck the people in wrath with a continual stroke, He who ruled the nations in anger, is persecuted and no one hinders."

Lucifer is persecuted by the high praises of God's people.

> "The whole earth is at rest and quiet; they break forth into singing."

We pray the day will come soon when the whole earth is singing perfected praise to God.

> *"Indeed the cypress trees rejoice over you, and the cedars of Lebanon, Saying, 'Since you were cut down, no woodsman has come up against us.' Hell from beneath is excited about you, to meet you at your coming; it stirs up the dead for you, all the chief ones of the earth; It has raised up from their thrones all the kings of the nations. They all shall speak and say to you: 'Have you also become as weak as we?'"*

Worship, to Satan, is like kryptonite to Superman.

> *"Have you become like us? Your pomp is brought down to Sheol, and the sound of your stringed instruments; the maggot is spread under you, and worms cover you.' "How you are fallen from heaven, O Lucifer, son of the morning! How you are cut down to the ground, you who weakened the nations! For you have said in your heart: 'I will ascend into heaven, I will exalt my throne above the stars of God; I will also sit on the mount of the congregation on the farthest sides of the north; I will ascend above the heights of the clouds, I will be like the Most High.' Yet you shall be brought down to Sheol, to the lowest depths of the Pit. "Those who see you will gaze at you, and consider you, saying: 'Is this the man who made the earth tremble, who shook kingdoms, who made the world as a wilderness and destroyed its cities, who did not open the house of his prisoners?' "All the kings of the nations, all of them, sleep in glory, everyone in his own house; but you are cast out of your grave"*

Lucifer, you will never have the rest that death could bring, because you will never die.

> *"Like an abominable branch, like the garment of those who are slain,"*

The garment of one who has been slain is bloody.

"Thrust through with a sword,"

The sword Lucifer is thrust through with is the high praises of God's people.

"who go down to the stones of the pit,"

Stones in a pit represent the lowest point of that pit, or what we would call "rock bottom."

"like a corpse trodden underfoot." (Isaiah 14:5–9, NKJV).

A dead person cannot keep people from dancing all over him or her. I believe this part of the judgment is accomplished when we rejoice, exult, and dance our praise to the Lord.

This Honor Have All His Saints

It is our privilege and honor as human beings—redeemed by the blood of Jesus—to execute God's judgments against the devil for as long as we are on this earth. The day will come when Satan will be cast into the lake of fire for eternity, but until that happens, we need to take care of our responsibility to God. We need to praise Him with all of our beings, holding nothing back.

We who are made in the image of almighty God—who are committed to His purposes for our lives—are the only ones who have the honor from God to punish Lucifer with our perfected praise. The angels do not have this honor. The stars and planets do not have this honor. The trees and the mountains can sing praise to God, but their praise does not punish the devil. The wild beasts, birds, and fish do not have this honor. Only the saints of God have been given the honor and privilege of carrying out God's written judgments against Lucifer.

If we do not do our duty on God's behalf, then Lucifer will run free all over the earth, causing pain and destruction. Let's bind him with fetters of iron! Let's keep him from doing any more damage—at least, in our parts of the world.

It is time for the saints of God to realize that God did not put mankind on the earth to be tormented by the devil. God put mankind on the earth to punish the devil for his sins. If anybody is going to make someone else hurt, it should be the saints of God, punishing the devil with high praises of God.

Just remember—if we don't inflict pain on the devil by praising and worshiping God the way He wants to be worshiped, then the devil will inflict pain on us.

> "Be sober, be vigilant; because your adversary the devil walks about like a roaring lion, seeking whom he may devour. Resist him, steadfast in the faith, knowing that the same sufferings are experienced by your brotherhood in the world. But may the God of all grace, Who called us to His eternal glory by Christ Jesus, after you have suffered a while, **perfect**, establish, **strengthen**, and settle you. To Him be the **glory** and the **dominion** forever and ever. Amen." (1 Peter 5:8–11, NKJV).

Concluding Thoughts

God has always had a way He wants to be worshiped. He has outlined that way for us in His written revelation—the Bible. In it, He has commanded us to worship Him with our entire beings, holding nothing back. This is the first and greatest commandment.

The reasons God has given us for obeying His commands to worship Him are because of who He is and because of what He does.

From His perspective, however, God's reason for creating a species of beings in His own image for the purpose of worshiping Him was to punish Lucifer for his sins.

Perfected Praise = **Biblical Worship**

Pastor Shamblin and Chris Stone in 2011

About the Author

Pastor R. Shamblin Stone

Shamblin Stone graduated from Friends University in Wichita, Kansas with a degree in Church Music and Voice. He has done graduate studies at the University of Phoenix in education.

Shamblin has served as the Director of the Music and Fine Arts Department of the Full Gospel Bible Institute in Eston, Saskatchewan. He has also helped start two other Canadian Bible colleges and served as their Director of Worship, Music, and Arts. These Bible colleges are the Christian Ministry Training Centre in Prince George, British Columbia and Evangel Bible College in Calgary, Alberta.

Throughout Shamblin's ministry, he has traveled extensively in Canada and the United States, holding worship seminars and serving local churches as a church music and worship consultant. He has served churches of all denominations, and has spoken at large conferences, and Bible camps.

Shamblin has distinguished himself as an award winning choir director. He has written worship songs which have been sung in churches around the world. Shamblin was the initial visionary of the "Worship Celebration", an annual worship conference held in British Columbia in the 1980's. Shamblin was a charter member of the steering committee for "Canada Arise," the national worship conference of Canada in the 1990's held annually in Calgary, Alberta.

After serving the Christian community in Canada for about eighteen years, Shamblin returned to Wichita, Kansas in 1999 to be near his mother, who was diagnosed with cancer. In 2001, Shamblin founded the Worship College in Wichita, Kansas, where he serves as the director.

Previous books authored by Shamblin Stone include Whatever Happened to the Prophetic Word? and Created for Relationships, both published by Neshamah Publishing of Calgary, Alberta. You Can Sing was published by SSM of Calgary. The Seminar of Biblical Worship was published by Vine Publications and Productions of Prince George, British Columbia. All of these books are currently out of print.

Shamblin and his wife Chris were married in May of 1973. Together they have four grown children, and they are raising two of their three grandchildren.

About the Worship College

www.theworshipcollege.com

Our mission statement is to teach biblical principles and worship leading skills which will enhance all styles of worship. We are not interested in changing your style of worship, but we want to help you make your worship the best it can be.

There are two tracks of study in the Worship College—the biblical track and the practical track.

Our practical courses are designed to equip every worship leader and worship team member with the skills needed to give worship leadership in his or her local church. The biblical courses are applicable for all Christians, to equip them to become the worshiper God created them to be.

Students can take both tracks of study online from anywhere in the world as long as they have a reasonable command of the English language. Visit our website for more information and to enroll.

Watch for the release of these Bible based Worship College text books coming soon.

- ➢ **Portrait of a Worshiper**—How and why we worship God as Individuals
- ➢ Principals of **Corporate Worship**—Examining the various Biblical dynamics of corporate worship
- ➢ **Leading Worship**—Biblical qualifications and equipping for primary and secondary worship leaders

Bibliography

Englishman's Strong's Concordance and Dictionary electronic text © 1993 OnLine Bible, 11 Holmwood, Winterbourne, ON N0B 2V0. All rights reserved.

King James Bible text is in the public domain except in the UK, where copyright is held by Cambridge University Press. Electronic text © 1995 Epiphany Software.

The American Heritage® Dictionary of the English Language, Third Edition copyright © 1992 by Houghton Mifflin Company. Electronic version licensed from InfoSoft International, Inc. All rights reserved.

The Living Bible, Copyright © 1971. Used by permission of Tyndale House Publishers, Inc., Wheaton, IL. 60189. All rights reserved.

Vines Expository Dictionary of Old Testament and New Testament Words, Copyright (c) 1940 W.E. Vine. All rights reserved. Material from Vine's Expository Dictionary of OT & NT Words is not to be reproduced in copies or otherwise by any means except as permitted in writing by Thomas Nelson, Inc. 501 Nelson Place, Nashville, TN 37214-1000.

The Holy Bible, New King James Version. Original work copyright © 1979, 1980, 1982 by Thomas Nelson, Inc. All rights reserved. Electronic Edition STEP Files Copyright © 1998, Parsons Technology, Inc., all rights reserved.

The Holy Bible: New International Version Copyright © 1973, 1978, 1984, International Bible Society. All rights reserved. Bible Source for Windows Version 2.1 Copyright © 1989-1995 The Zondervan Corporation. All rights reserved worldwide.

Common Era. (2012, January 1). In *Wikipedia, The Free Encyclopedia.* Retrieved 16:55, January 2, 2012, from http://en.wikipedia.org/w/index.php?title=Common_Era&oldid=468890960

Applied kinesiology. (2012, January 17). In Wikipedia, The Free Encyclopedia. Retrieved 07:48, January 31, 2012, from http://en.wikipedia.org/w/index.php?title=Applied_kinesiology&oldid=471823013